D1266724

BIBLIOGRAPHY AND TEXTUAL CRITICISM

Oxford University Press, Amen House, London E.C.4

GLASGOW NEW YORK TORONTO MELBOURNE WELLINGTON
BOMBAY CALCUTTA MADRAS KARACHI LAHORE DACCA
CAPE TOWN SALISBURY NAIROBI IBADAN ACCRA
KUALA LUMPUR HONG KONG

BIBLIOGRAPHY AND TEXTUAL CRITICISM

BY

FREDSON BOWERS

Alumni Professor of English in the
University of Virginia

THE LYELL LECTURES

OXFORD

TRINITY TERM 1959

OXFORD
AT THE CLARENDON PRESS
1964

FOR
NANCY HALE

One need not deny any man the comfort of belief arrived at by special revelation or intuition, by appeal to tradition or to any other authority greater than his own intelligence. But if he wishes others to share that comfort, he must give reasons that move the mind.

JOHN WILLIAM WARD
'Mill, Marx, and Modern Individualism'
The Virginia Quarterly Review
35 (1959), 539

FOREWORD

The six lectures that make up this book were delivered in Oxford University during Trinity term 1959 in my capacity as James R. Lyell Reader in Bibliography. The present text does not differ materially from the oral presentation except for the restoration of passages cut in deference to time limitations, and thus the lecture form of these discourses that in large part governed their original structure and tone has not been modified. However, I have welcomed the opportunity in my revision to add both reference and discursive footnotes which occasionally take account of pertinent scholarship published in the interval.

I make no pretence of having written any comprehensive or balanced account of the relationship between bibliography and textual criticism. My original plans had, indeed, envisaged a fuller survey; but when the lectures came to be written out for delivery, I must confess that the desire I had to deal at length with the nature of bibliographical evidence as applied to textual problems usurped my attention and dictated the path these lectures subsequently took. I regret the lack of a more systematic consideration—which is certainly needed—but the pressure generated by the subject turned my thoughts in another direction for these lectures.

In retrospect I think I can see that the pressure came from a strongly felt need to illustrate the nature of bibliographical thinking—the way in which the bibliographical mind works when tackling a problem and its evidence. Some experience with teaching the subject to graduate students has convinced me that techniques alone are very simple to convey. The bibliographer's tools are few and they can be taught in relatively short order. Their practical application to the solution of a problem is another matter, however; and here many a student goes astray from not having had the experience that long and painfully in the end shapes the attitude of mind that enables one to handle these tools to secure logical results.

Successful analytic bibliography requires a special frame of mind and a special way of thinking that can scarcely be dealt with in textbooks. Hence I found myself caught up in an attempt to look into the operation of the bibliographical mind as it approaches some problems of text. My original plans had contemplated a systematic explication of the principles of bibliographical research applied to textual criticism. The present lectures are manifestly not that, but something more personal: an attempt, perhaps, to get behind textbook rules and to trace the nature of the grooves along which the bibliographical mind pushes towards a solution of textual problems. This attempt is definitely not to retail the psychology of bibliographical investigation, but it is certainly more of an effort to discuss the rules than to formulate them.

It will be obvious—though the subject is technical—that the lectures were designed for an informed general audience such as is found in a university. Lectures do not encourage close bibliographical analysis in charted detail; hence, since it was method alone that was under consideration, I have drawn my illustrations from a narrow range of reasonably familiar material, chiefly in Shakespeare and the Elizabethan dramatists, and have often kept circling back to a textual or bibliographical example when the course of the argument could bring it up again in something of a new light. Since the examples are discussed only as illustrations of method and are without independent value, I have made no effort to offer fresh original research except in the final lecture, where I have presented concisely, as an illustration of a somewhat new technique, the provisional results of a compositor-study applied to the problem of determining the copy-text for the Folio *Othello*.

The numerous references to Dr. C. J. K. Hinman's monumental study of the Shakespeare First Folio derive from the privilege he extended me in 1957 and 1958 of reading his book in manuscript, and from the various discussions we had both then and earlier about the import of the evidence that he was to consider with such superb originality and clarity. Unfortunately, publication of his volumes was delayed beyond the point when my footnotes had to be written, and therefore page references to them are not made in this book. This lack should not be felt by the reader, however, who will be thoroughly familiar with the details mentioned from Dr. Hinman's work well before the appearance in print of my comments.

I gratefully acknowledge the support of a fellowship from the John Simon Guggenheim Memorial Foundation in 1958–9 that freed me from academic duties and enabled me to prepare these lectures.

F. B.

Charlottesville, Virginia
23 February 1963

CONTENTS

I

ANALYTICAL AND TEXTUAL BIBLIOGRAPHY

THE general procedures of textual criticism as it deals with manuscript study have been formulated for some years.[1] Differences of opinion may develop from time to time over the precise techniques for constructing a family tree from variant readings, and other matters of technical concern may occasionally come in dispute. But on the whole it is not unduly optimistic to suggest that when the editor of a classical or of a medieval text begins his task he can attack the problems from a position of strength. That is, he will be well aware that much drudgery lies ahead and that the difficult nature of the material may give him some bad hours; but he is seldom in doubt about the textual theories that guide him. Moreover, he can hopefully anticipate that if he follows these traditional methods for sorting out and arranging his texts, he will be left with few cruxes that cannot be solved by linguistic skill and ripe critical judgement.

In the halcyon days before the emergence of bibliography as a force, the textual critic of printed books could approach his task with something of the confidence of the manuscript scholar, fortified also by the comforting thought that, in comparison, the initial preparation of the text would be far less onerous. If he were the first adventurer, the number of early reprint editions to collate would not be large; and if he were a late-comer, he need only exercise his ingenuity in improving the edition of a predecessor, whose pages he

---

[1] The most convenient summary of the principles for dealing with manuscript texts is Paul Maas, *Textual Criticism*, translated by Barbara Flower (1958). For a shorter view, see 'Textual Criticism' (revised) in *Encyclopaedia Britannica* (1958 and later editions).

could send to the printer with an occasional correction. The choice of copy-text was not a particularly acute question, for what are now called the 'accidentals' of a text would all be modernized, and literary judgement could mend the errors in the 'substantives'.[1] Shakespeare's first known editor, Nicholas Rowe, used the precedent Fourth Folio, and Theobald based his own text on Rowe and Pope.

Even so late as the great Old Cambridge Shakespeare in the 1860's, the method had not been developed for distinguishing the original primary text from its piracy wrongly dated in the same year, evidenced by the selection of the Pavier Quarto of *The Merchant of Venice* as the authority superior to the true first edition. When two textual traditions were present, as in the Quarto and Folio of *Richard III*, the choice of substantive text would be referred to no other arbiter than literary criticism. The consistent modernization of all early texts solved many linguistic problems, for the serious anomalies created by such modernization were not as yet recognized.[2] As the form of an edited work was altered, so its texture was modified to agree with the expectations of contemporary readers, often in the general belief that it was being 'corrected'.

In short, optimism ruled, optimism and humanistic faith in the ability of literary taste to recover by successive refinements a substantially exact text for an author like Shakespeare. Any doubts could be traced to the fear that the extraordinary history of corruption of the Shakespearian texts at the hands of players and venal printers might still on occasion defeat the best unravelling efforts of the human

[1] These terms are drawn from the classic article by W. W. Greg, 'The Rationale of Copy-Text', *Studies in Bibliography*, iii (1950–1), 19–36.

[2] Nor are they fully recognized even today: see the debate between John Russell Brown, 'The Rationale of Old-Spelling Editions of the Plays of Shakespeare and his Contemporaries', *Studies in Bibliography*, xiii (1960), 49–67, and Arthur Brown's 'Rejoinder', ibid., pp. 51–76. The all-too-brief remarks of Alice Walker, 'Some Editorial Principles (with Special Reference to *Henry V*)', ibid. viii (1956), 109–11, are especially pertinent. Some consideration is given to the problem in Bowers, *Textual and Literary Criticism* (1959), pp. 117–40.

intelligence working through critical taste. As a consequence, the first series of bibliographical investigations of Shakespeare was aimed at the problem of the manuscript that stood immediately behind the print. The new experts found that the printer's copy was likely to be much more respectable than had been dreamed, perhaps even Shakespeare's autograph or an early official transcript of it. Thus the first impact of bibliographical research promoted even more heady optimism in clearing away one of the most serious doubts about the meaning of 'stolne and surreptitious copies' that had weighed for two hundred years on Shakespearian scholars.

Experts in a different field testify that a headache can be especially acute the morning after tasting *Heurige*, the new wine. So it may be that bibliographical second thoughts have produced some heaviness of spirit following on the initial glow of editorial optimism. The complex bibliographical attack on the problem of Shakespeare's text that has flowered after the Second World War has not as yet, perhaps, led to general disillusion, but it has certainly provoked critical confusion and sometimes latent resentment.[1]

The causes of this reaction are not far to seek. When a new and scientific scholarly method seems in its first application to conduct us to the verge of certainty, it is disheartening to find that the further development of the discipline does not fulfil the immediate promise that had been held out. From our present point of experience, for instance, it is genuinely sad to look back to the high confidence of a John Dover Wilson juggling the bolts of the New Bibliography like the hero of a Strauss tone poem. In his own day Wilson was read with genuine excitement, for he offered the certainty that appeared to lie in a new evidential basis for

---

[1] The resentment is not always latent: see Leo Kirschbaum, 'On the Editing of Elizabethan Texts', *Opportunities for Research in Renaissance Drama: The Report of Conference 23 (1959) and 20 (1960) of the Modern Language Association of America*, prepared by Samuel Schoenbaum (1961), pp. 13–20.

criticism. Now that we have been forced to recognize that his speculative textual insights will not stand up to present-day rigorous inquiry, we seek for a new prophet, but as yet no Aaron has come forward. Actually, current bibliographical research is moving ahead with astonishing speed, but its general effects tend more to show the specialist what he does not yet know than to open up new territory for exploitation by the general scholar. Each fresh bibliographical break-through only discovers more areas for technical investigation before criticism can begin to make use of the newer findings; and thus the day for practical application of bibliographical hypotheses on any large scale is continually being put off.

The general scholar, in the past, could follow the reasoning of a Pollard, and he could be vastly stimulated by Wilson's imaginative vistas. Wilson has recently described those early sunshine days as follows:

These discoveries [of the probability that Hand D in *Sir Thomas More* was Shakespeare's, and that many Shakespeare texts had been set from autograph or from early transcript] seemed to give good ground for a fair measure of optimism. It looked as if editors had only to decide, in regard to any particular text, whether it was printed from Shakespeare's manuscript, or from a prompt-book, and then proceed to edit it in the light of the newly acquired knowledge of how Shakespeare wrote, how he spelt, how he punctuated, and how at times he revised portions of the dialogue by making additions in the margin. But the situation [he adds] turned out to be far more complicated than was, or could be, realized at that stage.[1]

[1] 'The New Way with Shakespeare's Texts: An Introduction for Lay Readers. IV. Towards the High Road', *Shakespeare Survey*, 11 (1958), 79. For a delightful account of the early discoveries, see 'III. In Sight of Shakespeare's Manuscripts', ibid. 9 (1956), 69–80, and in some part 'I. An Introduction for Lay Readers', ibid. 7 (1954), 48–56. These reminiscences are of the most particular interest for the history of textual scholarship from shortly before the First World War to the outbreak of the Second. It will be noticed that, in the quotation given in the text above, the emphasis is on the exploitation of the newly respectable texts, as if the print were practically the equivalent of the lost manuscript. The complications that were to follow arose with the bibliographical realization that print and manuscript might differ widely in many details.

The complication of the situation so justly remarked by Wilson has led analytical bibliographers less towards conclusions that have an immediate and practical bearing on the solution of specific textual difficulties than towards a general attempt to lay the necessary factual groundwork for a new and more knowledgeable assault on the main problem. Hence the results of bibliographical effort to date have mostly been provisional, and they have appeared to offer little that a general scholar could actually apply in any useful manner to his own concerns. Was a given play quarto printed on one or on two presses, or on more than two? If on one press, was one skeleton, or more than one, constructed to impose its type-pages? Were the pages composed for the press in seriatim order or by formes from cast-off copy? Did one, or two, or more, compositors work on this playbook? Few critics or editors can imagine themselves contriving spelling tests or typographical analyses in order to identify compositors. Few have the training, or the interest, to apply technical information about printing to an estimate of textual variation and textual purity. That the detailed relationship of two or more editions and the exact facts of textual transmission can in complex circumstances be better settled by an analysis of concurrences as well as divergences in some hundreds of spellings instead of a dozen or so verbal readings and that an editor might be called upon to make this technical study, is a prospect so appalling as to lead to baffled rejection if not to disgust.

This is a world the critic never made, a world to which a sound classical education and a First in Greats seem to have little pertinence. The technical concepts explored and the bibliographical terminology required appear to be as remote from literary criticism as the language and concepts of linguistics or of a natural science. A remarkable activity seems to be in process, but to the general scholar it does not appear to be going anywhere. Few positive results that can be grasped seem to be produced. The bibliographers are prone to adopt a superior air about critical attempts to straighten out problems, and they are likely to advise critics to go slow or even to suspend all but the most peripheral of operations until bibliography has had a chance to tackle the matter. Yet often bibliographers appear to do no better than ordinary folk on problems that should be readily solvable if the technique fulfilled its claims. Was the Folio *Hamlet* set directly from a new manuscript or from a copy of the Second Quarto altered by collation with a manuscript? No answer has yet been provided so authoritative as to receive universal acceptance. One writer will believe that the Folio *Richard III* was set from an annotated copy of the Sixth Quarto patched with some leaves from the Third; another asserts that the annotated Third Edition was throughout the only copy-text; still another argues for shifting combinations of the First, Third, and Sixth Editions.

When those who are supposed to be the technicians disagree, what is a poor devil of an editor to do but plug ahead in the time-honoured way, using his critical judgement as final arbiter and hoping for the best. That he should proceed without some inner disquiet for the soundness of his results would scarcely be natural. Any day some stray bibliographer may come along and make a spectacular ass of him on a technical interpretation of the familiar evidence, or, as often, on newly dredged-up evidence that the critic could never know existed. Such a prospect leads more to wariness than to a friendly concern with the progress of this new scholarship. Indeed, it is a rare present-day critic who is not confused by the rapidly expanding bibliographical explorations. Editorial reaction is likely to be a throwing-up of hands. If the penalty for becoming an editor is the requirement to learn this new and greatly complicated technical discipline, most critics will have none of it. And, having none of it, they may be led to depreciate the claims of the specialized group that is invading the province of textual criticism.

Because this situation has its dangers for scholarship,

there may be place for a series of lectures, however brief, on certain problems of textual criticism applied to printed books, with special reference to the Elizabethan drama and to Shakespeare since so much research concentrates on this period. Although most bibliographical publication assumes the existence of these special problems, there may be some use for a résumé of their peculiar nature and, implicitly, for an indication of how these problems of printed books, especially in an early period, differ in important respects from the problems of manuscripts. Of more moment, it may prove useful to offer some analysis of what textual bibliography is all about. In this connexion, throughout these lectures I propose to emphasize the inquiry into the nature of the evidence on which textual bibliography operates, the logical forms of its reasoning, the techniques it uses, and the results it can achieve. This six-part study, then, attempts to explain and to illustrate the application of analytical bibliography to the main problems of textual criticism in a period of major interest, and to assess the value of the interpretation of the evidence afforded by its technical processes.

1. *Interpretation of Evidence*

Some years ago Dr. J. G. McManaway wrote: '. . . a Shakespeare drama is not one, but many plays: the ideal play as the author conceived it; the text as written; the tidied up fair copy, later marked and abridged for representation; the imperfect rendition on the stage; and the printed text or texts, that may represent one or more of these versions, either "maimed, and deformed", or "perfect in their limbs".'[1]

Some of these neither bibliography nor any other form of criticism can recover, for certainly we have no means of knowing what ideal form a play took in Shakespeare's mind before he wrote it down. But drawing on what is practicable here, we may say that the immediate concern of textual bibliography is only to recover as exactly as may be the form

[1] *Shakespeare Survey*, 1 (1949), 128–9.

of the text directly underneath the printed copy. When only one edition was printed, this recovery concerns the form of the manuscript from which the printer set. When there is more than one edition, it is the function of bibliographers, in addition, to trace the transmission of the text and thus to determine the sometimes complex forms of printer's copy used for editions after the first, whether a different manuscript, an annotated earlier edition, or an unannotated printed copy.

In so far as the determination of its form and details may offer evidence for critical hypotheses about the kind of manuscript used as the printer's copy—authorial, scribal, foul papers, fair copy, prompt-book, private transcript, or what not—these hypotheses may have a bibliographical basis. But I agree with McKerrow[1] in questioning whether much current inquiry into the transmission of the text prior to the printed form can properly be called 'bibliographical', although it is often assumed to be so. That is, the only applicable function of bibliography in such an inquiry is to attempt to distinguish which details of the printed text are compositorial and which are not, the purpose being to analyse the manner in which the printer's copy has been turned into print.

Such attempts to reconstruct the transition from printer's copy to book may involve complex investigations into the number of compositors who set the type, the number of presses that machined the sheets, the exact method of reading proof, and so on. These are essential in order to determine whether uniform or varied conditions obtained in the passage from manuscript to print, for criticism must not without evidence assume that the agents were necessarily the same and the processes always uniform. (Variable editorial criteria may need to be applied to different pages of the text according to the information revealed by this examination.) Thereupon, according to the uniform or to the variable conditions

[1] R. B. McKerrow, *Prolegomena for the Oxford Shakespeare* (1939), pp. vi–vii.

exhibited, an attempt may be made to strip the veil of print from the copy. The process involves isolation of the characteristics that may be attributed to the compositor so that whatever is left over may be examined for possible characteristics of the manuscript.

As a very small example, one may take an anomaly in the collaborated play *Lust's Dominion* (1657), a duodecimo. In II. i (as in I. iii) the Cardinal is called *Mendoza* both in stage-directions and speech-prefixes, whereas in II. iii he is not named but is *Cardinal* in directions and prefixes. Since II. i occupies sigs. C1–3^v, and II. iii sigs. C8^v–9^v, and there is no evidence for a change of compositors within the sheet, it follows that a difference in the manuscript is being reflected in the print. Further differences in scenes within this sheet C may be discovered. In II. ii 'Cardinal' as a titular reference in the text to Mendoza is in roman, as it has been in II. i, and 'Friers' is also in roman; yet in the next scene, II. iii (set by the same compositor), both *Cardinal* and *Friers* are set in italic throughout. The linked typographical change, therefore, seems to have taken place as a reflection of a difference in the underlying printer's copy between II. ii and II. iii.

Thus far strictly bibliographical evidence will take us. But it must be pointed out that if a critic uses this evidence to support an argument that the authorship of the play differs after II. ii, the interpretation is not itself bibliographical, even though the evidence on which it is based was bibliographically determined to be significant in terms of the characteristics of the printer's copy. The bibliographical interpretation, by itself, can seldom extend to the cause for the anomalies in the underlying manuscript, although it may provide the foundation for such a critical explanation.

This is a fundamental distinction that will often crop up in the discourse of these lectures; hence it may be as well to begin the relation of precept to practice here. It is a serious fallacy, I take it, to confuse the nature of the interpretation with the nature of the evidence. Sometimes the two will coincide, and the interpretation will be as bibliographical as the evidence, when mechanical evidence is interpreted in terms of the mechanical printing process. For instance, an examination of the running-titles of *Lust's Dominion* discloses that the text of the play in sheet B was imposed in two different skeleton-formes; but with the start of sheet C, and continuing to the end, the outer-B skeleton was discarded and only one skeleton-forme was used to impose the type-pages of both formes of the sheets. Whatever the significance of the change in the method of printing,[1] one point is clear: at least from sheet C on, *Lust's Dominion* must have been printed on only one press. It follows that we shall not have anywhere in the text such simultaneous typesetting of different formes or sheets as that which affects the text of Q2 *Hamlet* (1604–5) set by two compositors serving a pair of presses.

In the interpretation of the forms *Mendoza* and *Cardinal*, bibliographical reasoning on this limited evidence can carry us only as far as establishing that the variants are characteristic of two distinct literary units in the printer's copy, and are not the divergent practice of two compositors. Without first determining that sheet C was set by a single workman, no interpreter of the typographical evidence could draw any inferences at all in this respect that could properly be called bibliographical. For example, how differently uniform copy may be treated by two compositors is illustrated in III. iii, a scene that extends from sig. D11^v to E2. On sig. D12^v the speech-prefixes for the two friars appear in the forms *F. Crab* and *F. Cole*, but on sig. E1 when another compositor has taken over, the prefixes continue instead as *Crab* and *Cole*. Thus in the one example the bibliographer can recover

[1] Given the evidence, one can only guess. Perhaps sheet B was machined on two presses, but it is much more likely that starting with sheet C the typesetter found he was slower than the press and hence that there was no advantage to the use of two skeleton-formes. See 'Elizabethan Proofing', *Joseph Quincy Adams Memorial Studies* (1948), pp. 571–86. The *Lust's Dominion* problem is studied in *The Dramatic Works of Thomas Dekker*, iv (1961), 118–27.

variant characteristics of the lost printer's copy from the speech-prefixes; but, in the other, divergent prefixes in the print have no significance for the nature of the copy.

We come now to the heart of the matter. If a critic chooses to interpret the evidence of *Mendoza* and *Cardinal* in 11. i and 11. iii (and of the use of roman and italic in 11. ii and 11. iii) as indicating a shift from one to another of the collaborating authors, he is basing his hypothesis on bibliographical evidence; but the interpretation is not in itself a bibliographical one. The reason is not far to seek. The technical interpretation could extend only to the physical characteristics of the printer's copy. What actually caused this difference in the copy is quite another matter. So far as strict bibliography is concerned the difference might have been produced about as readily by a different scribe copying 11. iii from the scribe of 11. i and 11. ii as by a different author composing the scene, or else a reviser may have started his work with 11. iii. Thus no bibliographer in the practice of his discipline could properly attempt to deal with the prehistory of the printer's copy. Whether the bibliographically ascertained difference in the manuscript reflects a change of authorship, or not, is thereupon almost exclusively the decision of the literary critic working with questions of style and content.[1]

11. *Bibliography and Textual Criticism*

In so far as bibliographical analysis can emphasize immediately discoverable error, it leads without further consideration to specific textual emendation. Yet unlike the palaeographical method, which in its application to textual criticism seems to be concerned with specific and limited decisions, textual bibliography, at its most valuable, endeavours to investigate the general nature of the problem. The practice, or application, thereupon works out the formulated theory, and is limited by its terms. One of the soundest doctrines of textual criticism requires an editor to begin

[1] See note A, p. 30.

with the nature of the whole before turning to any individual part. In other words, the whole form must be determined before one comes to test any single word. The inquiry into the whole form may take different paths according to the circumstances. In a play first printed in the Shakespeare Folio, for instance, one is on sounder ground in proposing an emendation if one knows which compositor set the passage and what were his characteristics. Moreover, a decision about the nature of the underlying copy may act as a powerful determinant.[1]

Not least among the virtues of bibliographical analysis is the possibility it holds for promoting a climate of opinion about the compositor's relation to his copy that can have a long-range effect on textual emendation. For instance, the discrimination of purely compositorial characteristics that cannot be associated with copy may point up some details of the manuscript that can be compared internally or else can be put up against similar details recovered from other, perhaps associated, manuscripts. Notice may thereby be called within a print to significant similarities or dissimilarities in details that should be recognized by an editor. An editor of *Hamlet* may have his knowledge of the underlying copy for Q2 materially sharpened by observing how it is filtered through the variable characteristics of the two compositors, X and Y, within the quarto; and this information may be supplemented and checked by observation of the typesetting of these compositors in *Titus Andronicus* Q2 from printed copy and in *The Merchant of Venice* from manuscript. Moreover, even negative information is of value if it limits possibilities

[1] For instance, an editor's boldness is encouraged in *The Merry Wives of Windsor* by the working hypothesis that the Folio copy-text was several removes from autograph. As a consequence, he may admit more additions from the bad Q1 than he would be inclined to do if the copy had been autograph, in which case only compositorial blunders could presumably be repaired by reference to an inferior authority. Moreover, if the copy were non-autograph and derived from the prompt-book, an editor may emend *minutes rest* (I. iii. 26) found in both F and Q1 to *minim-rest* despite the concurrence of the only two authorities.

so as to prevent false hypotheses. Since the prints of the *Merchant* and *Hamlet* differ so markedly in their characteristics, though set by the same workmen, it is improbable that the copy for both plays was Shakespeare's foul papers, as formerly believed. A theory once evolved for each play in isolation from the other, and without regard for the agents who set the type, is now more than suspect. And if we conjecture that the copy for *Hamlet* was and the copy for the *Merchant* was not foul papers (indeed, perhaps not even autograph), editors of the *Merchant* may need to take another look at the general proposition that to date has directed their practice of emendation both in kind and in quantity. The climate of opinion will have changed.

Another sort of problem appears in *The Virgin Martyr* (1622) by Dekker and Massinger. Enough consistent spelling variation is present in the printed text, set by a single compositor, to provide quite enough evidence for assigning the authorship of every scene to one or other playwright. This evidence also suggests that authors' papers and not a levelling-out scribal transcript formed the printer's copy.[1] The textual critic can thus come to this text knowing the stylistic and linguistic characteristics of the two authors and aware that probably only one agent, the compositor, has intervened between holograph and print. His confidence in the authority of the underlying printer's copy can be high, and his estimate of the amount of hidden error in the print can be governed by what can be discovered about the specific compositor, not by what the editor imagines to be true of compositors in general. With this information the critic is in a very strong position to mend obvious textual error and to

---

[1] That is, not Dekker and Massinger as such can be identified bibliographically, but playwrights A and B. It is then the function of the literary critic to establish that A is Massinger and B is Dekker. In this play something of the prehistory of the printer's manuscript can be inferred from bibliographical evidence, although it is basically only a speculation that the manuscript must have been foul papers since the authorial characteristics noticed would not be likely to survive double transcription—by scribe and then compositor.

ferret out any hidden corruption. Nothing could be more valuable than the specific information he has received.

Bibliographical analysis can sometimes provide, as in this example, a general estimate of the soundness of the underlying copy. An editor is well advised to take such a general hint seriously even if he cannot always establish the exact mechanical relationship needed for the bibliographical solution of a specific textual crux. Whether he has or has not overall confidence in a text, or in some sections of it, is important. But it is even more important that bibliographical findings can set limits on the scope of a critic's conjecture and simultaneously can indicate the path that his reasoning must take. In *The Virgin Martyr*, for instance, a speculatively minded editor cannot blame corruption in the print on scribal error, memorial contamination by some theatrical agent, and so on through the list of fashionable scapegoats. He must deal with his authors and his single compositor. Thus in some circumstances an editor's whole estimate of the textual situation, both in general and in particular, can be strictly guided by bibliographical reasoning acting as a positive force on his decisions.

III. *Bibliography and Editorial Decision*

Whether conjectures about the origin and form of the printer's copy have a bibliographical basis is important to recognize. In her *Textual Problems of the First Folio* (1953) Dr. Alice Walker most ingeniously attempted to analyse the amount of compositorial error in the Folio *Richard III* by an extrapolation of the evidence of the two sections set from unannotated Q3. Then she attacked the problem of the number of erroneous agreements between the Folio and the Q1 text that are due to the oversight of the annotator who prepared the copy for Jaggard's workmen. By counting the number of errors that had developed between the First Quarto and what she took to be the main printer's copy, the Sixth Quarto, and then recording those that the annotator failed to correct, she was able to secure some percentages of oversight that gave her reason to believe that about 140 common Folio and Q1 readings represent concealed errors that should have been altered by comparison with the manuscript used for correction of the printed copy that served the Folio compositors. This useful information emboldened her in the text of her New Cambridge edition to more than ordinarily lavish emendation of shared readings. Certainly her method would appear to be basically sound in principle, and it has the virtue of giving the editor an unusually comprehensive view developed from bibliographical evidence in the text and its transmission.

On the contrary, in her *King Lear* study there can be no bibliographical basis for the speculation that the First Quarto was set from a manuscript taken down at dictation from foul papers, perhaps by the two boy actors who played Goneril and Regan. Her conclusion is that what was omitted from the Folio was never acted and must therefore be free from the errors caused by the chief agent relying more on his memory than on the manuscript from which he was dictating. This conjecture would have far-reaching consequences for an editor's treatment of the text, and it is therefore important to notice that the evidence offered in support of the hypothesis for dictation (even though casual) from an authoritative document, and especially the identification of an actor as the agent, is completely non-bibliographical. Whether one accepts or rejects the hypothesis, therefore, its validity for editorial procedure is markedly less certain than the validity of the bibliographical evidence in *Richard III*.[1]

Dekker's *Honest Whore, Part I* (1604) offers an example of editorial procedure deriving from bibliographical analysis.

---

[1] This is viewing the case narrowly, as what can be inferred by logical reasoning from mechanical evidence. Of course, a critical hypothesis like Dr. Walker's for *King Lear* may gain approval even though it is basically undemonstrable. But if we measure the validity of a working hypothesis by the concrete bibliographical evidence on which it is based, her editorial procedure for *Richard III* is better founded than her proposals for editing *King Lear*.

The analysis of the printing of the First Quarto showing that it was set by sections in three different shops turns out to be of vital importance in the interpretation of the text's transmission in the revised Second Quarto. In Q2 various formes were printed from standing type of Q1, and most of these, as well as the reset formes, exhibit substantive alteration of some kind, as well as changes in the accidentals. The major editorial problem is to determine the authority of the variants in both the standing and the reset type of the revised Second Quarto.

Once a critic is aware of the bibliographical divisions of this Second Quarto in relation to the First, he can see that a very marked difference exists between the variants found in the first bibliographical unit and those in the remainder of Q2. In the first section alterations that must be attributed to authorial correction and revision appear in the reset as well as in the standing type. On the other hand, in the later sections, although similar authoritative changes are made in the standing type, the variants in the reset pages are fewer and their nature is less certain. This anomaly can be interpreted by the hypothesis that the stationer sent to the printers a copy of Q1 that Dekker had annotated for a second edition. As this book passed from hand to hand the several printers altered their standing type in accord with its markings but did not note the annotations for the pages where they had distributed the type and not yet composed the reprint. The authorially corrected quarto at the end came to rest in the shop of the printer who had set the first section, and he was therefore able to retain it for use as the copy for his reset pages after correcting his standing type.

No alternative hypothesis appears satisfactorily to co-ordinate the bibliographical evidence. An editor is consequently encouraged to accept as authoritative all changes in standing type, wherever found, but none of the changes in reset type save for the substantives in the first bibliographical section. Application of the hypothesis thus makes editorial decision consistent and almost automatic. A workable editorial policy has derived from the discovery and then the interpretation of mechanical evidence.[1]

One critic whose acuteness was seldom betrayed, in this instance failed to grasp the essential connexion between the editorial decision and the bibliographical analysis. After complaining that 'a great deal of space is devoted to conjecture as to what alterations should be assigned to Dekker', he comments that the reader might 'get the impression that speculation is sometimes wasted on problems for the solution of which no sufficient grounds for evidence exist', and he adds, 'But after all, it is only on internal grounds that some alterations are accepted as coming from the author; and a sceptical critic might argue that here is a distinction without a difference, and that in all cases what the editor does, and all he can do, is to accept those changes that commend themselves to his judgement and reject those that do not.' 'I do not say', he concludes, 'that the critic would be right, but I think he might be rather difficult to answer.'[2]

The answer is, in fact, so easy that I am prepared to hinge these lectures on the proposition that when bibliographical evidence is properly analysed, interpreted, and applied to editorial problems, a distinction is produced that holds a difference very definite indeed. The whole point of the bibliographical examination of *The Honest Whore* was to provide evidence that there was an actual difference in the nature of the variants—according to the bibliographical divisions and according to no other principle. Internal grounds were used only to compare the evidence of the different bibliographical sections, and their texts, as units according to the physical fact of the reset or standing type. Once the critical faculty recognized that significant differences existed according to the physical divisions, bibliographical

---

[1] Further details appear in *The Dramatic Works of Thomas Dekker*, ii (1955), 4–15 and iv (1961), 409–14.

[2] W. W. Greg in *Review of English Studies*, N.S., vii (1956), 307.

reasoning immediately took over and altogether relieved the editor of the necessity to make decisions according as the individual readings did or did not commend themselves to his judgement. The variants in certain pages must be authoritatively based; in other pages, according to the bibliographical division, no variant could possibly have authority.[1]

What happens when a non-bibliographical editor approaches the same problem is well illustrated by the treatment given to this text in Hazelton Spencer's anthology *Elizabethan Plays* (1933), which is by usual standards a most carefully edited collection. The Second Quarto that contains the revisions had just been discovered, but Spencer knew of no systematic way to survey the variants and their authority. Hence although he selected a number of authoritative corrections from standing type, he had a general tendency to reject equally authoritative variants (according to our present knowledge) from the very same pages when they seemed relatively indifferent and therefore not to be truly required. Most serious of all, in the several major cases of rewritten passages in the text he refused to admit any of Dekker's revised intentions.[2]

As a result, Spencer's conventional eclecticism proved to be an untrustworthy editorial instrument since it was not based on a rational principle that derived from bibliographical evidence.[3] The difference between this and the bibliographical editing of the same play is most certainly an authentic one, for when the findings of bibliography set limits on the critical judgement by indicating the respective textual areas in which variants must be accepted and rejected, a true distinction was indeed produced.

This point is worth labouring because of the confusion

---

[1] See note B, pp. 30–32.

[2] The authoritative rewriting Spencer did not accept appears in II. i. 300–2, 444, 449, and 454. Some examples of authoritative readings he elsewhere rejected are *my naunts* for *mine aunts* (I. ii. 121); *thy* for *thee* (I. iii. 56); *no faith* for *in faith* (II. i. 35); *Whaat* for *What* (II. i. 38); *heed* for *heard* (II. i. 152). He rejected the correction *Malevolta* for the Q1 name *Malavella* at II. i. 91.   [3] See note C, p. 32.

that is sometimes generated about the relation of critical judgement to bibliographical evidence. To disbar critical judgement from the editorial process would be an act of madness, for there will often come a time when literary criticism is necessary to assist in the interpretation of bibliographical evidence. A brief look at some problems of press-correction will illustrate with suitably neutral examples. When only one forme of a sheet is variant, there will usually be, apart from the variants themselves, no bibliographical evidence to indicate the order of printing the respective states of the forme. If an editor is fortunate, one state may exhibit some literal errors such as turned letters, types obviously transposed, and so on. The natural inference follows that these errors called forth the appropriate corrections (not the reverse), and that the state containing the errors is therefore the earlier.

In so far as the corrected errors are typographical and thus separate themselves in their kind from literary alterations involving a choice of meaning or an improvement in the method of expression, the decision about the order of the two states is doubtless 'bibliographical'. If this is so, then substantive readings in the same forme cannot be critically evaluated in a manner independent of the bibliographical. That is, regardless of what seems to the critic to be the direction of change in the meaning of the press-variant words, such inferential evidence can have no validity in comparison with the impersonal concreteness of mechanical, or typographical, variants in demonstrating the order of correction.[1] Press-correctors do not deliberately introduce typographical errors in the copy, but they will not infrequently introduce verbal error through misconstruction. Hence meaning is a treacherous guide to the direction of change, especially if it is assumed that the critically preferred reading must be the later, whereas in most circumstances mechanical evidence capable of bibliographical assessment is trustworthy.

[1] See note D, p. 32.

Copious observation establishes that mechanical alterations made during the printing of a forme are always
designed to improve the typographical presentation of the
inked impressions. Dr. Hinman's records of the number of
times a First Folio forme might be stopped in press for
minor typographical adjustments are very illuminating.
Hence it may be taken as a sound bibliographical principle
that one should assume the direction of mechanical changes
to be towards correction, and that the distinction between
what is a lesser and what a greater state of mechanical
correctness is not usually subject to opinion. No such
certainty can exist when we come to assess textual changes in
the readings. The intent of the press-corrector was undoubtedly to correct error, but his execution was sometimes so
wayward as either to corrupt an authoritative reading or else
to substitute one form of error for another, like the proof-
reader of Dekker's *Westward Ho* (1607) who at 1. i. 90
altered *wist* to *means* when *wit* was in fact required. With
very few exceptions, therefore, the relatively impersonal
evidence on which bibliographical analysis flourishes may be
interpreted in mechanical terms to give a reliable answer,
whereas critical decisions about the direction of change may
be arguable because the basis is not fixed.

On the other hand, if the question is one of authority, and
not simply of temporal sequence, bibliographical techniques ordinarily have no pertinence applied to the isolated
problem whether certain variants were introduced on the
proof-reader's own responsibility, or whether they resulted
from reading proof back against copy or from the writer's
own intervention.[1] Whether or not any single variant is more

---

[1] Occasions will arise, however, in which bibliographical logic will set limits to
critical conjecture. Thus if an authoritative press-correction is found in the inner
forme of a sheet, the bibliographer will insist that some further physical connexion
be established before this occurrence is taken as affecting the evaluation of the variants in the outer forme, or in some other sheet. It may happen, as with half-sheet L
in Dekker's *Match Me in London* (1631), that what at first appeared to be one set of
authoritative press-corrections, on further bibliographical examination turned out

than technically authoritative involves a value-judgement that bibliography is not equipped to give. For instance, in Dekker's *Match Me in London* (1631) an uncorrected state reads as follows:

> *King.* Whom hast thou poyson'd?
> *Doctor.* The Queenes Father.

When the proof-reader altered 'Father' to 'Father in law' (a character that does not exist), a critic is justified in taking it that the wrong meaning (which is the later) is sufficient factual evidence that someone other than the author made the change.[1] But if we treat these two readings in a strictly bibliographical manner as inked shapes with no meaning, as in a strange foreign language, then any reliance on bibliographical techniques to tell us which an editor should accept as the more authoritative would be met with silence. Only after the values-judgement has been made and the lack of authority has been critically established can bibliography resume its interpretation of the evidence.[2]

Thus in the case of *1 Honest Whore* the bibliographical examination established certain fixed divisions in the play that represented groups of sheets printed in different shops. Within these divisions it separated the pages in standing type from those in reset type. Only then, and within the limits of these physical distinctions, was the editor's judgement invited to examine the variants in the standing type of the different sections. The critical decision followed that in each section the formes of standing type contained at least

to be two sets, made at different times; hence the authority of one group could not be transferred to the other, even though they appeared in the same forme.

[1] Of course, forgetful authors can introduce such errors into their correct original text. In this instance, however, the error is not an isolated one but part of a series that reveals a most unusual proof-reader at work.

[2] In addition, if this reading had been isolated in the forme, the bibliographer probably could not have told the critic the demonstrable order of the two variants, for any inferences would need to be based on the critical assessment of the meaning in the absence of mechanical evidence.

some variants that could not be attributed to the printer's initiative and gave every sign of authorial instigation. Bibliographical logic then stepped in again and required the editor in his application of this information to accept all such variants in standing type, significant or indifferent, with no option to pick and choose among them unless some real error could be inferred.[1]

The pages of reset type were critically surveyed according to the bibliographical divisions of the sheets printed in different shops. In the first section a number of variants were found in the reset type that were identical in their nature with the variants in the standing type. Bibliographically, any of these that could not be imputed to the compositor had to be treated for editorial purposes in the same manner as the variants in the standing type. According to the critical view, the variants in the reset type of the remaining bibliographical divisions differed in their kind not only from those in the reset pages of the first section but also from the variants in the standing type of the later divisions. A simple conclusion to draw was that these variants were unauthoritative. Bibliographical logic then instructed the editor to accept no variant in these pages as if it were an authoritative correction or revision. This was a blanket order, leaving the editor without the very small option he could exercise in the acceptance of the variants from standing type.

When we survey this reconstruction of the editorial process with its logically derived, consistent results stemming from a factually based principle, and make a comparison with conventional, unsystematic editing like Spencer's, guided by the critical judgement alone, it should be obvious that a gulf lies between them. A valid distinction must be recognized between eclecticism referring for confirmation only to literary taste as a source for each individual decision, and the manner in which bibliographical scholarship makes

[1] See note E, pp. 32–33.

use of the critical judgement under controlled conditions and thereafter establishes the limits within which this judgement can operate eclectically in its application to editorial problems and their solution.

Another case-history of this sort occurs in Dekker's *Match Me in London* (1631). Here bibliographical investigation first establishes a physical connexion between the printing of the first and the last half-sheet gatherings of the quarto, and then between the various stages of press-correction in both half-sheets. Having connected these phenomena, the editor brings his judgement to the problem of whether any one of the linked sets of press-corrections seems to differ in its kind from the others in these two half-sheets and, in addition, from any set of the numerous variants throughout the quarto. When in his critical opinion one set from each half-sheet fulfils these conditions, and when these two sets are then discovered to be bibliographically related since they were made at the same time in the same forme, the basis is laid for the argument from analogy that the author himself ordered this one group of press-corrections but (so far as can be told) no others in the book.[1] Again, bibliographical regulation in effect marked off the problem for the critical judgement. Even though it was only on internal grounds that one group was selected as very possibly authorial, the bibliographical conditions to the selection were stringent enough, and the application of the decision rigorous enough, to remove the editorial decision from all suspicion of eclecticism based ultimately only on personal taste.[2]

---

[1] That the set in half-sheet A concerned details of the author's dedication perhaps explains his unique intervention in the text of half-sheet L.

[2] Eclecticism, of course, means only the practice of selection and is not necessarily to be equated with mere personal taste or lack of principle. Indeed, modern editorial eclecticism deriving from logical textual and bibliographical principles has won out over the old-fashioned conservative diplomatic-reprint school to which scholars in the past were driven in their opposition to really unprincipled eclecticism. For some remarks on scholarly eclectic editing, see *On Editing Shakespeare and the Elizabethan Dramatists* (1955), pp. 69 ff., and *Textual and Literary Criticism* (1959), pp. 101 ff.

iv. *Analytical Bibliography*

Bibliography concerns itself with books treated as tangible objects. This is a truism. But, truism or no, the baldness of the statement has led to various misconceptions. The analytical bibliographer examines books as tangible objects in order to recover the details of the physical process of their manufacture. This general method starts with historical study: what can be gathered about the printing process from external evidence such as printers' manuals, contemporary references, trade records, and what not. Then by an independent investigation the student endeavours to recover exact details about printing methods in general by scientifically analysing the physical evidence of the books themselves—what may usually be called, in comparison, from internal evidence. Next he may endeavour to apply the knowledge thus gained in order to interpret—from specific evidence in any given book—the effect of the production process on the physical characteristics of this book, considered as part of an edition, and of any of this edition's variant copies that comprise impressions, issues, or states. Finally, this analysis of the effect of the production process on the physical characteristics of a specific book may be developed in one of two ways, either as the foundation for descriptive bibliography, or as the foundation for textual bibliography, both of which serve as intermediaries between the book and the textual or literary critic.

Dekker's *Match Me in London* offers a case-history, already mentioned, that may be somewhat elaborated here as illustration of these four steps. First, from printer's manuals we know that two half-sheets may be machined separately, each as a unit, by the 'work-and-turn' method. Or else a forme from one may be imposed with a forme from the other for printing, the two remaining formes for perfecting, and the full sheet then cut in two, the halves representing one copy each of the two different half-sheets.

As the second step, when we examine quartos to recover evidence that will distinguish the two methods, we find that the evidence of the watermarks is significant if enough copies are preserved. The consistent division between watermark and no watermark in a number of copies usually shows when two half-sheets in a book are pairs originally machined together in a full sheet; or the random clashing of water-marks in the two half-sheets will indicate that each was imposed and printed separately. But another method may exist if a running-title is present in one page of each forme of either half-sheet. Under these conditions, a stricter form of bibliographical evidence can decide which method of imposi-tion was employed according to the pattern of transfer of these two running-titles from earlier formes.[1]

Thirdly, when we come to apply this evidential method to *Match Me*, we find that the running-titles prove that its two half-sheets A and L were indeed machined together, and the combination of the running-title pattern and the appearance of more than one round of press-variants in both half-sheets shows that inner A was imposed with outer L, and vice versa, as printers' manuals often illustrate. Complete confirmation for the imposition of the formes in this manner was afforded by the collimated light from the Martin Lamp, which demon-strates mechanically which side of a sheet is the first printed and which the perfected forme.[2]

The importance of establishing the formes that were imposed together is made clear when these press-variants are examined. One group ordered at the same time in both half-sheets is seen to contain characteristics that differentiate it from press-alterations ordered elsewhere in the quarto and especially from alterations that were made a little later in these very two formes, apparently by the regular corrector of the

[1] 'Running-title Evidence for Determining Half-Sheet Imposition', *Studies in Bibliography*, i (1948), 199–202.

[2] For the principle of this lamp and its operation, see K. Povey, 'The Optical Identification of First Formes', *Studies in Bibliography*, xiii (1960), 189–90.

quarto.[1] This correlation of evidence may then be used as the basis for a critical hypothesis that the author was the agent for the correction of this single group of unique variants. A number of indifferent accidentals that no editor would otherwise accept as authoritative (certainly not on literary judgement alone) may therefore be admitted by a bibliographical editor as part of his reconstruction of the most authentic and exact text possible. In little, the two half-sheets of *Match Me* exemplify the four sequential steps by which evidence from the production process may be brought to bear on textual problems embodied in the physical characteristics of a specific book: that is, historical study, the determination of actual printing methods from internal evidence, the correlation of information from these two sources to solve a given concrete bibliographical problem, and the final application of the solution to textual criticism, or editorial decision.

v. *The Nature of Textual Bibliography*

The determination of the physical, external form of a book in terms of the technical analysis of its production is the function of analytical bibliography applied to description. This process does not collide in any direct manner with other forms of analysis, such as those that go by the name of criticism. But the relation of analytical to textual bibliography, and thence—immediately—to textual criticism, *is* subject to misinterpretation, principally because analytical bibliography thereby invades a field that has customarily been pre-empted by some form of literary criticism. Hence, once we broaden the concept of what bibliography actually represents, we may see that 'the examination of a book as a tangible object' applies to something more than the formal description of a book as a dimensional thing without relation to its contents. In truth, the same analytical bibliography that enables us to draw up a permanent description of the external

---

[1] These variants, and an analysis, may be found in Dekker's *Dramatic Works*, iii (1958), 254–5, 259–61, 348, 356–7.

form of a book is, in another connexion, equally concerned
with the internal form—the contents. The application to
external form identifies the discipline of descriptive bibliography. The application to internal form, or contents, is the
concern of textual bibliography. Through this subdivision of
its pure form, analytical bibliography thus becomes a partner
in the process of textual criticism.

The peculiarity of the approach of textual bibliography is
this. The contents—the author's words—are not treated
primarily as symbols instantaneously to be resolved into
meaningful concepts in the mind. Instead, at least at the
start, the words and punctuation are thought of primarily as
simple inked shapes, imprinted on paper from pieces of
metal systematically selected and arranged by some human
agent, the compositor. This point of view leads to another,
and perhaps less familiar, concept of the book as a tangible
object, in which internal and external form imperceptibly
merge into one. Accordingly, the function of textual bibliography is to treat these imprinted shapes, their selection and
arrangement, without primary concern for their symbolic
value as conceptual organisms—that is, not as words that
have meaningful values—but, instead, as impersonal and
non-conceptual inked prints. Thus the general laws governing the setting of the pieces of metal and their transfer of
tangible inked impressions to paper are the very real concern
of the bibliographer.[1]

To determine the exact details of the mechanical process
that produced the sequence of these inked shapes, and the
prior selection of the order of each metal shape within the
sequential arrangement, is the chief end of textual bibliography. In other words, the heart of the method consists in
supplying a mechanical explanation for all mechanically
produced phenomena whenever such an explanation can be
arrived at on the recoverable evidence. The transfer of in-
scribed symbols in a manuscript to the forms of impressed

[1] See note F, pp. 33–34.

symbols in a book is a mechanical process; hence, any explanation that can be made within the terms of the mechanical operation for phenomena relating to these transferred symbols is ordinarily to be preferred to explanations that ignore the process and seek some other terms of reference. This is the simple difference between a bibliographical and a critical explanation. The one seeks the causes of mechanically produced phenomena in the production process itself; the other assigns reasons for the phenomena that are historical or literary and thus ultimately refer to values, or opinion, as the basis for judgement.

A brief reference back to the press-variants in the two half-sheets of Dekker's *Match Me in London* will illustrate. A non-bibliographical critic ignorant of the mechanical connexion of the first-stage variants in inner A and outer L could attempt to associate them only by arguments for their similar nature, and at best these arguments could merely be persuasive, never what might be called demonstrative. But the analytical bibliographer, concerned simply with how these variants were produced, can indeed come close to demonstration by mechanical evidence that the alterations in the pages of inner A were made at the same time as those in outer L and therefore by the same agent. Whether this agent was or was not the author is a question that the bibliographical method alone cannot attempt to solve. Yet without referring at all to values, as to whether these variants seem to be superior, or more tasteful, the textual bibliographer can point out that in relation to the other press-corrections in the book they are uncharacteristic, in one particular respect, and that in a later round of alteration in these very pages a number of quite characteristic changes *were* made in press. The natural inference is that the agent who ordered the first round differed from the agent who ordered the second, and that only this second agent could reasonably be identified with the regular proof-reader whose operations were visible elsewhere in the book. But beyond this factual, non-values judgement, the strict bibliographical method cannot go without encroaching on other territory and using another order of evidence—that of literary judgement applied to textual criticism. Such critical judgement is often necessary; indeed, it may be said to be ultimately necessary in the editorial process. But it operates according to different criteria and can be appealed to only after the bibliographical evidence has been exhausted and the process completed of analysing and then interpreting the mechanical phenomena according to mechanical criteria.

One cannot repeat too often that when the evidence of analytical bibliography can be made available, literary and historical judgement must be limited by bibliographical probabilities and must never run contrary to mechanical findings. Impersonal interpretation is invariably to be preferred to personal interpretation when the facts are present necessary for the construction of an acceptable hypothesis; and the mechanical interpretation of the bibliographer, based on physical fact, *is* to be preferred to the subjective interpretation of the literary critic from taste and another order of experience. When bibliographical and critical judgement clash, the critic must accept the bibliographical findings and somehow come to terms with them. Critical assumptions can never be so demonstrable as strict bibliographical interpretation from sound factual evidence. Indeed, this is not a question of degree: when a clash develops, strict bibliographical method must be assumed to be right, since step by step it rests on the impersonal interpretation of physical facts according to rigorous laws of evidence. And, correspondingly, criticism must be wrong, since its interpretation of evidence can ultimately rest only on opinion, or common consent in matters of taste governing judgement.[1]

This being so, a particular responsibility must be placed on bibliographical research to make sure that its method is strictly observed in order that accurate results will be

[1] See note G, pp. 34–35.

achieved. Otherwise, very disturbing consequences may follow acceptance of faulty interpretation of bibliographical evidence offered with exaggerated pretensions to authority. In this matter it cannot be said that all of our textual critics are blameless. Attempted bibliographical reasoning may be used too lightly as a speculative stalking-horse without sufficient factual basis. To put it plainly, the bibliographical method has been abused, sometimes in carelessness, sometimes in ignorance and sometimes in cynicism when it is treated merely as one of the arts of persuasion.

Indeed, unless bibliographical discipline can be better controlled in the future than it has been in the past when applied to textual problems, the general literary critic may be very well advised to view its claims to positive results with some protective reserve.

NOTES

Note A, p. 11. So Philip Williams by observing the change (independent of the stints of Compositors A and B) of the form *Burgundy* in Acts I and II of *1 Henry VI* to *Burgonie* in Acts III–V was able to infer that two different hands had been concerned with the manuscript that served as printer's copy; but the bibliographical evidence that was sufficient to substantiate this discovery was not of a nature to suggest whether one or other of these hands was Shakespeare's, or whether the differences in forms between the first two and the last three acts had any significance for an investigation of the authorship or whether they were only scribal. See 'New Approaches to Textual Problems in Shakespeare', *Studies in Bibliography*, viii (1956), 3–14. The problem of the manuscript behind Q2 *Romeo and Juliet* (1599) has been interestingly investigated by George Walton Williams. Once more the uniformity of certain details within the typesetting of two different compositors is taken as evidence for the hypothesis that these details were characteristic of the underlying manuscript. Then when these details change within the work of one compositor, the ground is laid for the hypothesis that the nature of the manuscript changed too. In this case the difference is taken to be only that between fair copy and foul papers. See Dr. G. W. Williams's unpublished University of Virginia dissertation on the text of *Romeo and Juliet*,

Note B, p. 18. If a confusion were to arise in connexion with this example, it could centre on the process by which the variants in certain pages were initially recognized as authoritative. Here, of course, the critical judgement established, first, that variants of a certain kind were found in all the formes of standing type, whereas—except in the opening section—variants of this kind were not found in the formes of reset type. Many of the variants in the standing type could be reasonably imputed only to an authoritative source. Only one or two variants that might have belonged in this group appeared in the reset pages of those sections after the first; and thus a control revised section could be isolated according to a bibliographical unit. In the Simmes formes, whether standing or reset, the variants were largely homogeneous, and this homogeneity extended to the variants in the standing type of the other bibliographical units but not to their pages of reset type. True, some readings in the standing type were as indifferent as a number of readings in the reset pages. But once, bibliographically, these could be associated in the standing-type formes with manifestly authoritative readings, the mechanical conditions of their production required them to come from the same authoritative source—and one's literary judgement found nothing inherently objectionable in the association. On the other hand, similar indifferent readings in the reset pages could not be associated bibliographically with readings of comparable authority such as those that were frequent and prominent in the Simmes control pages. Since these reset readings were generally of the nature one would expect to find in reprints, no difficulty obtained in assigning them as unauthoritative. Actually, no more internal evidence was used than is found in any critic's judgement that, as a bibliographical unit, the First Folio represents a revised version of the basic Q1 text of *Richard III*, whereas the Second Folio, as a bibliographical unit, represents a mere reprint without the infusion of fresh authority. The analogy is inexact only to the extent that the F1 revision was more complex than that in *1 Honest Whore* Q2 and thus that the conditions approximate to those in the reset Simmes pages, where corruption could enter from the fresh composition. The alteration of standing type, of course, pinpoints the exact changes made and reduces very materially the opportunities for corruption stemming from the compositor. Without the distinction between the reset and the standing type a critic trusting only to his judgement would almost certainly have been puzzled about the exact status of the relatively indifferent variants throughout the play, as was Hazelton Spencer (see below, and p. 18, n. 2). The bibliographical hypothesis that 'explained' the reasons for the odd state of affairs was useful but not crucial for the operation of the editorial principle. To sum up, it was the function of criticism to take the readings of each bibliographical unit *as a whole* (according to standing-type and reset formes in each printer's section) and to come to some conclusions about the authority or non-authority of the significant variants susceptible of critical decision. Thereafter, bibliographical reasoning prevailed and prevented critical picking and choosing among the variants in each category of a section. They were either all authoritative or all non-authoritative, in the nature of the bibliographical case. This general statement does not prevent acceptable corrections (not revisions) from appearing in the reset pages, and some errors of commission in the standing pages, of course (see note D below).

Note C, p. 18. Critical eclecticism is no mean instrument in the hands of an expert, as witness (say) the Old Cambridge text of *Richard III* that imports the Folio reading into the faulty Q1 copy-text in almost every place where a marked clash in meaning develops. Nevertheless, the problem of the 'indifferent' reading—one where the meaning seems to be so equally balanced between two variants that one might as well toss a coin—by its nature defeats the eclectic approach and so produces the principle: Follow the copy-text when in doubt. Since not every authorial alteration will be manifestly superior to its original form (as we know from *1 Honest Whore*), the principle of 'follow the copy-text' is only playing the odds. This is what Spencer did, with generally good but by no means with altogether accurate results. The peculiar virtue of the bibliographical editing of *1 Honest Whore* was that it solved the stubborn problem of the indifferent variant in a manner not otherwise possible, since it was able to use a mechanical means of separating the page-units that were simple reprints from those that had undergone authoritative revision.

Note D, p. 19. Granting, of course, the absence of mechanical accident such as the movement of loose types, pulled type improperly replaced, or pie followed by resetting, that might create typographical error in a sheet that passed through the press later than a correct one. The errors in the resetting of part of a pied forme in Dekker's *Roaring Girl* (1611) are instructive (*Dramatic Works*, iii, 4–5), especially since the present writer was originally misled about the order of settings because of his bibliographical ignorance. If we move from press-correction and its consequences to simple resetting, then there is no bibliographical principle to assert that a mechanically more correct state is ordinarily the later. Indeed, what appears to be the mechanically less perfect typesetting of the Preface to Dekker's *Sun's Darling* is very likely the later (*Dramatic Works*, iv, 4–9). This is no academic question, for an editor must find reasons for selecting the more authoritative state set direct from manuscript.

Note E, p. 22. Error could be of three major kinds: (1) The author might inadvertently have made some slip that was faithfully reproduced, or he might, perhaps through haste, have misunderstood his own original. Such an authorial misunderstanding may have occurred in the repunctuation of i. v. 221–2 (cf. *Dramatic Works*, ii, 111–12), and an authorial slip in the substitution at i. v. 121 of *We are* instead of *We're* for *Were* (ibid., 10 n.). (2) The compositor may have incorrectly set the author's markings. At i. v. 129 it is probable that a comma is a mistake for an apostrophe. (3) Some agent in the printer's shop may have added his own corrections to those of the author, thus mixing unauthoritative with authoritative alterations. The possibility of this action is in some part related to the physical circumstances. If the author presented the shop with a list, it might be that the agent who copied them on a proof could feel impelled to alter what he regarded as additional authorial oversights. But in the reconstructed circumstances for *1 Honest Whore* in which we may conjecture that the standing type was corrected from what would correspond to Dekker's own marked proof, the chances for interference from someone in the shop would seem to be materially lessened. Moreover, it is less likely that a compositor charged with making corrections would bother about reading proof and inserting further alterations on his own initiative. In *1 Honest Whore* at ii. i. 204 a suspicious alteration was made, and at ii. i. 215 another for which the reason is by no means clear. These seem to be just about the only variants in standing type that might cause an editor any worry. On the other hand, the standing type of sheet F somehow escaped substantial correction, perhaps because it was type transferred from one shop to another between the printing of Q1 and Q2, and here the two very minor alterations that appear in the standing type are very likely a printer's concern, unless they are representative of press-correction in a lost state of Q1. One variant merely replaces a comma after a speech-prefix with a full stop, a mechanical alteration. The other adds *and* before the last of a series of names in a stage-direction. Since no clear-cut authorial revisions were available for this particular set of type-pages, it is likely that someone in the shop took it upon himself to read them over for errors that he could spot. We need not necessarily suppose that just such small printer's variants also appear in the standing type of sheets that are not anomalous, since the conditions appear to have differed. It follows that even under such ideal mechanical restrictions as govern the editorial policy in treating variants in the standing type of *1 Honest Whore*, the critical judgement cannot be completely neglected, for two or three such alterations in Q2 must be rejected by an editor. Nevertheless, such rigid scrutiny was required by the bibliographical evidence before any altered reading could be ignored as to remove the editing quite completely from the pick-and-choose method that a non-bibliographical editor would be forced to adopt. If the choice of Q2 variants were not, in fact, altogether enforced in an automatic manner, it was so nearly automatic—after a critical survey of the bibliographical implications—as to make small distinction. Certainly the confidence with which the bibliographical editor could approach the nasty problem of the indifferent reading in this play contrasts remarkably with eclectic dis-ease.

Note F, p. 27. The concern of the analytical bibliographer with the precise selection and arrangement of types brings in the study of compositors in a manner not always appreciated. Too often the analytical bibliographer has seemed to concentrate on problems of press-work and of the general manufacture of the book after the initial stage of composition. This concentration is understandable, since the procedures involved in the post-composition manufacture are most applicable to the elder sister, descriptive bibliography. Moreover, greater certainty is usually possible: the rules for handling the arrangement of type-pages on the press and the physical process of impressing sheets of paper from these inked type-pages are fairly rigid, logical, and thus predictable for analysis. The postulate of normality can be relied on with some confidence, even though one's trust may not be absolute. (See, for example, the later discussion of the order of perfecting sheets in relation to their printing.) In contrast, the uniqueness of each compositor, and of his mental and physical habits and reactions, lends to the detailed study of his work an unpredictable basis in which the human equation is often of the first importance. In many significant ways each compositor is a law to himself, subject to all the irrationality associated with human operations under individual responsibility. As a result, his typesetting as it manifests itself in the transmission of the contents is sometimes illogical and therefore difficult to analyse. The postulate of normality is usually impossible to apply to a given problem with an absolute rigour. These difficulties have long discouraged the bibliographical analysis of the compositorial operation and have, indeed, caused some resistance to accepting the validity of post-war pioneering studies. Not all critics are convinced that spelling-tests will indeed identify compositors, or that a close study of their individual habits of transmitting the characteristics of their copy is at all practicable. Fortunately, both processes are indeed workable, as first-hand experience, instead of theoretical scepticism, will demonstrate. The chief difficulty is the mass of material needing to be studied and the extraordinary amount of time required for even the simplest analyses.

    Note G, p. 29. For example, the first-stage variants in the two half-sheets of *Match Me in London* are not altogether uniform in their kind. A critic might conceivably choose to argue that certain differences in these variants in half-sheet L from those in half-sheet A reflected a difference in their origin and thus that two agents must have been involved, one for each half-sheet. This is an example of what may be called personal critical interpretation, since it ignores the mechanical production of the press-alterations in hypothesizing a distinctive physical basis for a difference in the variants that (without physical evidence) has been assumed to be significant. On the contrary, the bibliographical approach to the problem may be called impersonal, since it concerns itself only with the mechanical production of the variants. Having ascertained that the alterations appeared in type-pages within the same forme and therefore in the same proof-sheet that would be pulled for the reader to scan, the bibliographer decides that the one agent must have marked the pages for correction in both half-sheets. This decision is non-literary and impersonal: it disregards the nature of the variants and therefore hypothesizes that—whatever their kind—they must have been ordered by the same agent (*a*) because they are found in pages from the same proof-sheet, and (*b*) because they were made in the type at the same time by the compositor to whom the proof-sheet was delivered. Therefore they may be assumed to have originated in markings made at the same time on this proof-sheet. The hypothesis for one agent does not rest on the nature of the variants at all (a question involving personal taste) but on the impersonal ascertaining of the mechanical method of their production. On the contrary, a literary critic could use only his personal estimate of the nature of the variants to argue on the one hand for a single agent, or on the other hand for two agents.

II

THE TREATMENT OF EVIDENCE

1. *Inductive versus Deductive Reasoning*

THE relation between the bibliographical and the critical interpretation of textual phenomena, and the preference for the bibliographical in cases when mechanical explanation can be derived from sufficient and appropriate evidence, are important matters worth more scrutiny than they have generally received. The problem is mainly one of defining the areas in which bibliography and criticism can properly co-operate to produce the ideal whole—for the ideal is, indeed, a synthesis of the two, or at the least a complementary partnership. But a distinction between the two methods is also necessary, for bibliography has its own laws of evidence that must be observed, else its way is being violated.

If we are to prefer a mechanical explanation to any other for problems susceptible of mechanical solution, we must demand that such an explanation conform to the laws of bibliographical evidence. One of these laws requires us to reason inductively from specific, concrete evidence in the text.[1] When there is insufficient evidence to support inductive reasoning, pseudo-bibliography will usually result if (as a substitute for specific evidence) we try to deduce an interpretation of textual phenomena from our general ideas about printing practice.

A frequent offender in this respect is J. Dover Wilson when he employs a conjectural method that is quite improper

---

[1] I am aware that *inductive* and *deductive* as applied to reasoning have acquired philosophical half-lights that may in the end cause a subtle mind to deny that there is any difference between them. I am not happy about my need to use these terms, and I hope they will be accepted in just the rough-and-ready, practical sense intended by Bacon.

for any form of bibliographical reasoning. Typical of the dangers are his hypothetical reconstructions in *The Manuscript of Shakespeare's Hamlet*, i. 134 ff., of various errors in Q2 *Hamlet* as the result of a compositorial anomalous spelling or misreading followed by faulty correction from the proof-reader. For instance, in Q2 Claudius informs Gertrude at III. i. 32–33, 'her father and my selfe,/*Wee'le* so bestow our selues' whereas the Folio reads, '*Will* so bestow'. Wilson takes it that the Q2 *Wee'le* was a miscorrection not of a Shake-spearian, but of a compositorial, spelling which included such forms as *well* for *will* and *tell* for *till*. The only pertinent statement he makes about these anomalous forms is this: 'there is a tendency for "will" and "till" to be spelt "well" and "tell" '. But when we examine Q2 we find that as against 160 *wil(l)* spellings there is precisely one *well*, and this one occurs in a context that strongly suggests the compositor thought it represented a pun on the adverb *well* rather than the auxiliary *will*: 'if it be not to come, it will be now, if it be not now, yet it well come' (v. ii. 231–3). We find also that as against 16 *til(l)* spellings there are two of *tell*: 'Ile leaue you tell night' (II. ii. 571), and 'Tell then in patience our pro-ceeding be' (v. i. 322). Both of these last appear to be legiti-mate; but one suspect *well* as against 160 *will*, and even two *tell* as against 16 *till* forms is not altogether the 'tendency' that Wilson discovered without the supporting evidence that would have subjected his statement to the cold light of fact.

There is no evidence, then, that can be considered seriously to support Wilson's reconstruction deriving *Wee'le* from *Well* (= *Will*) in preference to some other explanation, such as simple memorial failure, if we are to take it that *Wee'le* is indeed an error, a matter of some doubt. On the contrary, if one wants to consider the matter bibliographically, instead of imaginatively, evidence can be found that makes Wilson's theory for the origin of an error even more completely im-possible. Wilson misconstrued non-bibliographical evidence and decided that only one compositor set Q2. Now, from strict bibliographical evidence, we know that two compositors were employed in the quarto, and we can identify the exact pages that each workman set.[1] We find that the one example of *well* (whether or not it is legitimate) occurs on sig. N3^v; the first example of *tell* is on F4^v and the second on N1. Each of these three pages was set by Compositor X, and together they comprise Wilson's total evidence. But, unfortunately, the passage in which Wilson thought that an original compositorial *Well* spelling was the basis for the error *Wee'le* occurs on sig. G1^v, a page set by Compositor Y. Thus even if there had been a 'tendency' for *will–till* to be set as *well–tell* (which there was not), this would have been a characteristic only of Compositor X. Not even a shred of such evidence exists in the play to associate a *well* (= *will*) spelling with Compositor Y, who set the passage in question. So much for guess-work.

Because this faulty *well–will* hypothesis is then used as the basis for another reconstruction, one may cite a further example of the folly of applying a veneer of bibliography to disguise what are actually critical guesses. At I. iii. 83 Q2 reads, 'The time *inuests* you', whereas the Folio appears to have the true reading, 'The time *inuites* you, goe, your seruants tend'. The Q2 error *inuests* Wilson conjectures to have come from a compositorial spelling of manuscript *inuites* as *inuets*. The press-corrector, he supposes, then attempted to lend an air of plausibility to an incomprehensible word by adding what he thought to be the missing letter. *Inuets*, therefore, was altered to *inuests* in an unrecorded state of proof-correction.

This reconstruction may sound very 'bibliographical' to the uninitiate, since it appears to explain an anomaly in terms of a mechanical process. But actually it does no such thing according to any kind of bibliographical reasoning. Wilson's deductive hypothesis is the product of guess-work without

---

[1] John Russell Brown, 'The Compositors of *Hamlet* Q2 and *The Merchant of Venice*', *Studies in Bibliography*, vii (1955), 17–40; and F. Bowers, 'The Printing of *Hamlet* Q2', vii, 41–50, and viii (1956), 267–9.

evidence in the text to support it. His deduction comes by analogy from two assumptions. First, in seven known formes of this book a press-corrector did alter certain readings, at least some of these representing outright sophistications without reference back to the printer's copy. The second assumption is improper since it is based on a false analogy: because *tell* can be a doublet for *till* (and much less certainly *well* for *will*), it does not follow, as Wilson suggested, that *inuets* is an analogous and possible doublet for *inuites*.[1]

From this general idea of printing practice (the existence of press-correction in Elizabethan printing), and an incorrect linguistic assumption, Wilson deduced an explanation for a textual difficulty. How void of concrete evidence the case is, and how entirely a product of the imagination, is obvious on the most elementary analysis. We have no evidence that the compositor would, or did, set *invites* as *inuets*. (*Till–tell* is no proper analogy; and even it if were, we should still want evidence that *inuets* was the form originally set.) We know that the proof-reader read the forme of inner C in which this line occurs, for a single alteration is found on sig. C3^v and another one on C4, the page that contains *inuests*. It is not impossible to conjecture that a lost earlier state of press-correction had been made in this forme: such successive stages are known in general printing practice, and indeed outer N in this same quarto had two corrections made in a second round of alteration as against seven for a first round. But we have no evidence for a lost state of press-correction antecedent to the preserved variants in inner C; and indeed bibliographical probabilities might suggest the contrary.[2] Even if we were to take the plunge and to accept the possibility of earlier press-correction in the forme, we are still a long way from any specific evidence to suggest that if

---

[1] *Inuests* occurs on sig. C4, which was the work of Compositor X, who had set the two *tell* and the one *well* forms. But the linguistic situation is altogether different for *inuets*: after all, there is no analogy between the substitution of short *e* for short *i* and for long *i*. [2] See note A, pp. 59–60.

the word *inuites* had been set as *inuets*, then the proof-reader altered the word. That he sophisticated a few other words from among the thousands in the quarto can scarcely be used as evidence to suggest that he did so here, else we could as readily blame on him any other Q2 error we wished to select. In short, no evidential basis exists for inductive reasoning that could bring to bear bibliographical analysis on the word *inuests*. If one must deduce an explanation, simple misreading by the compositor is much more plausible than the pyramiding of hypothesis required by Wilsonian speculation.

In the absence of any evidence that the proof-reader touched the word, or that the compositor set it originally as anything but *inuests*, it is not only pointless, it is dangerous to contrive such speculations. Wilson's attempted explanation, therefore, has no more validity—because it is cast in language that refers to the printing process—than if he had framed it in the critical terms of value-judgement. It takes more than bibliographical language to achieve the bibliographical method. It takes bibliographical evidence.[1]

II. *The Nature of Factual Evidence*

Bibliographical evidence must be identified with concrete, physical evidence if the principle is to hold that the peculiar value, and indeed the essence of bibliography is that it treats books exclusively as tangible objects. Yet to insist that hypotheses should have a factual basis is by no means to draw a distinction between a critical and a bibliographical interpretation. When critical interpretation essays the explanation of textual phenomena, the phenomena in question are facts, after all, since they exist in the form of inked shapes impressed on leaves of paper. In textual criticism some sort of a physical fact is always present at the heart of the inquiry. Hence the difference between the critical and the bibliographical explanation lies in the laws governing the treatment of the evidence by which the fact is investigated, an interpretation

[1] See note B, pp. 60–61.

formulated, and a solution for the problem finally proposed. The distinction lies not in the nature of the phenomena to be explained, therefore, but in the method used to derive the explanation. Criticism cannot avoid treating these inked shapes as meaningful symbols with literary values. Bibliographical analysis, at least at the start, tries to treat them as significant in the order and manner of their shapes but indifferent in symbolic meaning. Consequently, critical investigation can treat the phenomena in a text on internal grounds as self-sufficient evidence, whereas the method of bibliography usually requires supplementary evidence to support its interpretation of the phenomena.

One caveat must be entered. It is a requirement of bibliographical investigation, though a need not always felt by literary critics dealing with text,[1] to investigate any textual 'fact' carefully to make sure that it is a whole fact. I am not now referring to the conclusions that are drawn from an examination, or from a lack of examination, of existing evidence; but instead to the determination of the accuracy and completeness of the evidence itself before conclusions are attempted.

For example, it is certain that two compositors set the Second Quarto *Hamlet*, although Wilson 'proved' the presence only of one. His was a wrong assumption proceeding from a faulty interpretation of only a small part of the evidence that actually existed in the text, and to that extent his criticism was based on incomplete facts. Nevertheless, the point to be emphasized here is that the incomplete factual basis for his interpretation was not caused by any real lack of physical evidence in such bibliographical concerns as running titles, different founts of italic type, and even varying spelling-patterns. Instead the damage was caused by his faulty principle of selection from within the text of erroneous readings deductively presumed to be compositorial; and when these seemed to be uniformly scattered throughout the play, the

---

[1] For some horrid examples of criticism led astray by failure to check the facts about the details of its texts, see my *Textual and Literary Criticism* (1959), chapter 1.

conclusion was drawn that only a single workman could have produced such evenly distributed error. All the necessary facts that resided in the inked impressions were there for Wilson if he had seen their significance, just as they were there for the later bibliographers who recognized and correctly interpreted the mechanical evidence. In like manner, the confusion about Compositor B's characteristics in the Shakespeare First Folio, and the failure before Dr. C. J. K. Hinman's researches to distinguish him from Compositor E, were caused not by any lack of the necessary spelling distinctions but by faulty interpretation of a body of facts about the spelling that, as it proved, should have been sufficient to reveal the truth.

A recent example of careful investigation aimed at recovering all the facts and testing their significance before an interpretation is ventured is Dr. W. C. Ferguson's study of one of Valentine Simmes's compositors.[1] This piece of research is doubly interesting because it shows the extraordinary value of mechanical evidence in preventing just such mix-ups as have occurred about the spelling characteristics of Folio Compositors B and E, and of A and C and D. Dr. Ferguson noticed that in the First Quarto of Shakespeare's *2 Henry IV* (1600) in all but 5 of the 335 occurrences of unabbreviated speech-prefixes no full stop or other punctuation appeared, whereas a stop regularly closed an abbreviated prefix. Very scrupulously he did not assert that this might be significant evidence until he had tested the twenty-eight plays printed in the years 1599 to 1601 and found that only four full prefixes in the group were unstopped, all the rest being punctuated as if they were abbreviations.

Confident now that he had a distinction that was a difference, he examined the occurrences of these unstopped

[1] 'The Compositors of *Henry IV, Part 2, Much Ado About Nothing, The Shoemakers' Holiday,* and *The First Part of the Contention*', *Studies in Bibliography*, xiii (1960), 19–29.

prefixes in 2 *Henry IV* and found that they were uniformly distributed throughout the text. The problem then posed itself: was this a shop practice or the characteristic of a particular compositor. Examination of other typographical details such as the use of italic or of roman for names, titles, territories, the sparing use of emphasis capitals and of round brackets, suggested that the text of 2 *Henry IV* had been set by one compositor only; and this hypothesis was strengthened by other mechanical evidence such as the uniform positioning of stage-directions, the use of lower-case instead of capitals to head exit directions, and the invariably brief treatment of catchwords. However, these still might reflect severely imposed shop practice. Hence before all this mechanical evidence could be interpreted as identifying a specific compositor, a spelling analysis of the text had to be made. When certain preferential spelling forms were found to be evenly distributed through the text, the conclusion was reached that only one compositor set 2 *Henry IV*.

Confirmation of the evidence in 2 *Henry IV* is provided by the uniform appearance of the same characteristics in Simmes's quarto of *Much Ado About Nothing* (1600). Still, the evidence does not permit a firm decision whether the mechanical facts reflect Simmes's shop practice (if there were any such thing in Elizabethan printing-houses) or an individualistic compositor's preferences. Thus it was significant that in Simmes's Quarto of *The First Part of the Contention* (1600) the text in the formes of inner and outer A and outer B exhibited contrasting mechanical characteristics to those for the other sheets of the quarto, which had been set by the compositor of 2 *Henry IV* and *Much Ado*. Unquestionably another workman had started the play, to be replaced by the compositor who had been identified; and this distinction between the identified workman and another compositor was also to be observed in the Simmes Quarto in 1600 of *The Shoemakers' Holiday*. The conclusion could then be drawn with confidence that all of the observed mechanical habits of the *2 Henry IV* compositor, including his use of unstopped full speech-prefixes, were individual habits, and not some hypothetical shop practice; hence they could be utilized to distinguish his work from that of Simmes's other compositors. The case is an admirable one and admirably worked out in the testing of the validity of each piece of the physical evidence as truly a significant fact until a coherent and demonstrable hypothesis could be formulated in terms that one could presume to be complete.

As a contrast we may take a case of a different order (since it concerns a single, precise reading) where the physical evidence, when only partly known, would lead to quite erroneous conclusions if an investigator failed to make a maximum effort to determine its completeness. Three copies of Q2 Hamlet read at v. i. 321, 'An houre of quiet *thereby* shall we see', whereas the Folio reads 'An houre of quiet *shortly* shall we see'. The Q2 reading *thereby* is a textual fact, right enough, for this is the shape taken by the inked impressions in three of the preserved copies. However, if a critic were to decide between the Folio and Quarto readings on this evidence alone, he would be operating from what is actually an incomplete factual basis, because the other three preserved copies of Q2 read *thirtie* instead of *thereby*. This reading *thirtie* is found in the uncorrected state of the outer forme of sheet N and thus represents the sequence of types that was originally set by the compositor. It is bibliographically clear that *thereby* is the proof-reader's alteration, and critically that it is his rationalization of *thirtie*, without reference to copy.

Thereby makes some kind of sense, although not much question exists that the Folio's *shortly* is superior. However, it could easily happen that a conservative critic, determined whenever possible to defend readings from the Second Quarto, might find himself arguing for *thereby* as authentic if he knew only the three copies with this reading, whereas he could not have argued for *thirtie*. Of course, *thereby* cannot be regarded as authoritative once the whole fact is known and the distinction made between the original and the press-corrected inked shapes.[1] Once we learn that *thirtie* was what the compositor set, we may discuss with the palaeographer whether the Folio variant *shortly* might have been misread in the Q2 manuscript as *thirtie*; and on the affirmative the critic may adopt the Folio reading with some confidence as a well-authenticated one: first, as what we must assume to have been the reading of the manuscript used in the preparation of the Folio text;[2] and, second, as very likely the reading that stood in the manuscript behind Q2. By the analysis of the complete set of facts, the critic may be led to the choice of reading that, in Greg's acute summary, 'strikes a trained intelligence as supplying exactly the sense required by the context, and which at the same time reveals to the critic the manner in which the corruption arose'.[3] The reasoning from evidence is very different indeed from the unsatisfactory speculation about *inuests–inuites*, and particularly about *Wee'le* and *Will*, in which Wilson indulged himself.

This same corrected forme of *Hamlet* Q2 contains another interesting problem of the same sort. In the un-corrected state, on the page with *thirtie*, we read,

> Our indiscretion sometimes serues vs well
> When our deepe plots doe *pall* (v. ii. 9–10),

but the proof-reader altered this *pall* to *fall*, seemingly on his own responsibility. Editors choose *pall* customarily since it

---

[1] That this distinction between knowing the whole set of facts, or only a part of them, is not an academic matter is well illustrated by C. J. Sisson, *New Readings in Shakespeare*, ii (1956), 227: 'Folio reads *shortly* for *thereby*, rightly followed by editors. Unlikely as it may appear, *shortly* can well be misread as *thereby* in rapid writing.' Mr. Sisson has here ignored the bibliographical point or been unaware of the press-correction. Unless we are to assume that the proof-reader referred to copy and misread what he saw there (and we have no evidence that he did so refer in correcting this forme), whether *shortly* could be misread as *thereby* is not in question. The compositor of Q2 did not set *thereby* from manuscript: he set *thirtie*.

[2] See note C, p. 61.

[3] W. W. Greg, *Principles of Emendation in Shakespeare* (1928), p. 5.

is what the compositor of Q2 set from manuscript, and it is the reading that appears in the Folio.

However, depending upon the copy for the Folio *Hamlet*, the Folio's apparent confirmation might be of little worth. For example, if F *Hamlet* were set from an annotated copy of Q2, divergence between them that one cannot impute to the three Folio compositors who were engaged in the play must be the transferred reading of the manuscript used for comparison. If one is to adopt this hypothesis about the transmission of the text, bibliographical logic permits no other assumption (save, perhaps, misreading by the annotator). On the other hand, agreement between the two texts *may* mean that the Folio manuscript shared the identical reading with Q2, or it *may* mean that the annotator did not observe a divergence from his manuscript and therefore the Folio compositor followed his Q2 copy in a reading wherein the manuscript behind the Folio actually differed. Some shared readings like 'the dead *wast* and middle of the night' (I. ii. 198), or 'being a *good* kissing carrion' (II. ii. 182), or 'sanctified and pious *bonds*' (I. iii. 130), have been explained on this latter basis by editors who wished to emend them.

Hence if the joint Q2–F reading of *pall* were to be attacked, the sceptic would have little argument if the Folio were set from a manuscript throughout, for *pall* would be independently confirmed. But he could certainly have an arguable case (in the sense that the physical conditions do not discourage the conclusion) if the Folio were set from an annotated copy of Q2, for under such circumstances the editorial position would be much more flexible. However, one proviso would remain: only if it could be shown that the copy of Q2 used for the Folio had the uncorrected state of outer N with the reading *pall* could oversight by the Folio annotator be conjectured to explain away a shared reading. Otherwise, if the corrected state with *fall* had been the copy, we should be as sure that *pall* came from the Folio manuscript as we should be if we knew that the entire *Hamlet* Folio text

had been set direct from manuscript without reference to Q2.
It is fortunate that no objection is made to *pall*, for the evidence is insufficient to decide whether the Folio was set from
the corrected or the uncorrected state of outer N (assuming
that Q2 was the copy). Thus an interesting textual question
that bibliographical analysis might easily have solved from
a survey of the whole facts about both corrected and uncorrected readings fails of definitive answer for want of
crucial evidence about the printing process (i.e., the state of
the Folio copy-text) from which one can reason inductively.[1]

It is clear that a critic who does not work from bibliographically analysed texts risks basing his conclusions about
precise textual points on incomplete facts, although in the
nature of the case he does not realize that they are incomplete.
This is a different matter from the dangerous critical practice
of using any reprint at hand without recognizing the powerful forces that corrupt a transmitted text. The critics of our
earlier literature are by this time pretty well indoctrinated
in the use of first editions,[2] or else in the use of what may
be called bibliographically prepared texts.[3] It is chiefly the
critics of post-Renaissance literature who may sometimes be
led to formulate their appreciative analysis not on the author's
words but on a misprint in a faulty text, and thus on what
may also be called an incomplete fact.

On the other hand, especially in early books, the use of any

---

[1] It is disappointing, of course, that an answer cannot be given to a problem of
such general bibliographical and textual interest. The discussion here is aimed at
examining the nature of evidence and its treatment, however, and not at solving
a series of problems out of hand, agreeable as it would have been, of course, to have
offered a solution.

[2] See note D, p. 61–62.

[3] A bibliographically prepared text will have collated a sufficient number of
copies of any substantive edition to discover the majority of cases of press-alteration
that produce internal variance in the readings, such as the important *thirtie–thereby*
variant in Q2 *Hamlet*. It will also have examined the authority of all editions that
could have any claim to the title and it will have systematically utilized such
authoritative revisions and corrections as can be established in these editions. Needless to say, it will have correctly ordered the editions and identified the one or more
that were set directly from manuscript.

copy that comes to hand of a first edition may be dangerous for textual criticism concerned with specific readings, as in the examples above from *Hamlet*, unless sufficient collation has established the complete knowable facts about the variants in the inked shapes that were created as part of the proof-reading during the course of printing the sheets. The need for textual critics to know the whole of the basic facts before any interpretation can be made extends, indeed, beyond the question of individual readings and into the very choice of texts itself. The bibliographical determination that the Pavier Quartos of Shakespeare were misdated revealed that the Old Cambridge editors had based their text of *The Merchant of Venice* on an unauthoritative reprint. In a sense, also, the Old Cambridge editors' choice of the inferior bad quartos of *Richard III* and of *King Lear* over the corrected Folio texts was due to an insufficient determination of the facts about textual transmission, and it is only of late years that critics have studied Marlowe's *Doctor Faustus* in a text of superior authority to that of the bad quarto, which had been the editorial standard. Until the facts about the relationship of any two substantive Shakespearian texts are determined, an editor has no sound bibliographical guide for evaluating the concurrences, or the variants, in texts like *Hamlet*, *Othello*, *2 Henry IV*, or *Henry V*.

An example of the need to establish the facts about the relationship of two sets of inked impressed shapes before textual decision can operate comes to hand in Dryden's *Wild Gallant*. Not until 1922 was it discovered that two editions had been printed in 1669 and hence that there was a problem to determine their order and to isolate the true first edition. How sadly textual critics can be led astray when a bibliographical basis for decision is wanting may be illustrated by George Saintsbury's mishap. By bad luck this eminent critic got hold of the second edition when he came to re-edit the Scott Dryden; and under the illusion that he was purifying the Scott text, he substituted various of the second edition's unauthoritative corruptions for the relatively correct Scott readings based on the 1701 Folio set directly from the true first edition.

When one comes to collate the two 1669 editions of *The Wild Gallant*, comparison of some eight copies establishes that what we are to recognize as the true first edition had had at least seven press-variant formes, and that the reprint, or second edition, had been set from an example with six of these formes in their corrected state. This series of facts is enough to establish the order of the editions. If the order were reversed, we should be forced to the hypothesis that the proof-reader compared his proof directly against copy (an unusual procedure for a reprint) and in that reprint marked for correction only certain cases where his proofs differed, without making a single independent alteration not found in his copy. This theory is so remote from all known practice at the time as to constitute sufficient evidence in itself, without appealing to the single piece of impersonal bibliographical evidence that is alone quite enough: a misreading in the second edition which is the direct result of a faultily inked letter in the first. Here then is a case where the knowledge of the whole facts about the existence of differences among the inked shapes in one text was applicable not alone to the question of the best specific variant readings within the only authoritative edition. As a bonus, knowledge of the facts permitted the demonstration of what indeed was the true authoritative edition set from manuscript and thus enabled an editor for the first time to establish the exact physical form of the text for this play.[1]

One of the difficulties the present-day textual critic encounters is the requirement to keep up with the ever-expanding bibliographical concept of what constitute the necessary facts about the physical evidence of a text. I have remarked earlier that when Dover Wilson came to examine

---

[1] 'The First Edition of Dryden's *Wild Gallant*, 1669', *The Library*, 5th ser., v (1950), 51–54.

whether a single compositor, or several workmen, set Q2 *Hamlet*, he knew no other test than to evaluate what he took to be substantive errors; and when in his opinion they proved to be uniformly distributed, he accepted this evidence as sufficient to show that only one compositor set the text. Technical evidence from bibliographical analysis has, fortunately, overturned this critical estimate and established the truth from a broader view of what constitutes evidence, or what are the necessary facts to survey in coming to a decision on such a question.

For some years critics have been able to utilize a small group of strongly variant spellings in Shakespeare's First Folio to separate the work of Compositors A and B. But in a manner scientific beyond anything ever before attempted in the application of analytical bibliography to textual criticism, Dr. Hinman has now identified the five compositors who actually did set the type for the Folio. His evidence takes habitual spelling patterns only as confirmation for the much more precise and powerful evidence of the cases of type used by each compositor as identified by the shifting concurrences of hundreds of identifiable imperfect types traced from setting and distribution to setting again, all through the Folio. Thus physical evidence never before apprehended now plays a crucial role under some conditions in the important process of identifying the workmen through whose hands (and heads) passed the transmission of much of Shakespeare's text. Our view of the physical facts resident in the pieces of metal that impressed the Folio's inked shapes has now been greatly expanded by the invention of this new analytical technique.[1]

III. *Bibliographical Treatment of Evidence*

When a textual critic has determined what the facts are about the inked shapes that make up his text, and whether these shapes are variant or invariant, only then can he proceed to the bibliographical interpretation of his facts. At this

[1] See note E, pp. 62–63.

point, without elaboration, I should like to point out the latent confusion that is possible in any discussion of what constitutes a fact. For my present purposes I propose to limit the word to physical evidence alone, and to divorce it from any connexion with the interpretation of this evidence. For instance, it is a physical fact that the place in which the action of Dekker and Massinger's *Virgin Martyr* is laid is spelled *Cesarea* in some scenes and in others *Cæsarea*, and that the two spellings are never mixed in one scene. That this spelling difference, combined with other spelling and punctuation differences, distinguishes scenes written by the two authors is not a physical fact in the same sense but instead is a hypothesis. If the hypothesis comes to be generally accepted after considerable testing, the authorship of the different scenes may be accepted as factually demonstrated. Certainly, one can remark, such evidence of unconscious authorial spelling habits is a more factual base for hypothesis than a critic's general feeling for individuality of style, or the usual laborious attempts to prove authorship by parallel passages. Nevertheless, the generally accepted 'fact' that Massinger wrote certain scenes and Dekker others is of a very different order from the physical fact that *Cesarea* in one or other spelling appears in certain definite scenes.

That some pages of the Shakespeare First Folio exhibit uniformly a strong preference for the spellings *doe, goe, here,* and other pages a strong preference for the spellings *do, go, heere,* is a concrete fact, of course, demonstrable by arithmetic rather than by opinion. However, the moment that interpretation enters, one must stop talking about facts in the same terms. If the evidence is profuse enough to be significant, and consistent enough to be valid, one can have a particular confidence in the hypothesis that when such opposing characteristics as these are confined to bibliographical units and do not reflect literary divisions, different compositors have been revealed by the varying spellings. The hypothesis is factually, not impressionistically, based and is likely to be accepted as the only possible interpretation that can explain the evidence in a reasonable manner. Just so, Dr. Ferguson operated with the evidence connecting one of Simmes's compositors with unstopped full speech-prefixes.

Bibliographical interpretation of such physical facts has its own laws of evidence that differ from those customarily employed by literary criticism. Two matters, especially, distinguish the interpretative method of textual bibliography from that of other disciplines: the kind of evidence sought, and the method of interpreting this evidence. The bibliographical inquiry begins by determining the precise details of the mechanical process that produced the inked shapes under examination. It then concludes by endeavouring to establish a relationship between these precise mechanical details and any phenomena among the inked shapes requiring explanation. To the degree that such a relationship can be established within the three orders of bibliographical evidence and its interpretation (what is demonstrable, probable, or possible), a bibliographical explanation for textual problems is practicable.

Something of a myth has arisen in the popular mind that 'bibliography' is all-embracing and invariable; that all bibliographical interpretations of textual problems are, or should be, of equal and even of absolute authority. Nothing could be farther from the truth. It may often be that the practitioner of analytical bibliography can determine with overriding and even absolute authority the general details of the mechanical process by which a particular book was printed. That is, under most conditions, in the pre-Restoration period one may discover with fair certainty whether a given book was typeset by one or more compositors and printed on one or more presses, just as it is known that the pseudo-Marlowe *Lust's Dominion* (1657) was set by three compositors but printed on only one press. A bibliographer can often determine the order of formes through the press, establish the conditions under which press-correction would have operated (as in the difference between a book printed with pages set seriatim and one, like *Match Me in London* [1631], set by formes from cast-off copy), and even identify—in some instances exactly—the pages and part-pages set by a given compositor, on the evidence of the cases that he used. But the authority with which analytical bibliography may perform this general analysis of physical evidence cannot always be matched by the authority of the textual bibliographer in relating this ascertained physical evidence to an interpretation of minute features of a printed text, especially to details of any given reading such as would be the ultimate concern of an editor.

It may be that analysis can recover with considerable exactitude the conditions under which the inked shapes comprising a text were given a physical existence, as Dr. Hinman can do in astonishing detail from his study of the Folio types. But this is only the first step, and it does not necessarily follow that our knowledge of these conditions can always be used with equal authority to explain textual phenomena. Everything rests on what exact relationship the textual bibliographer can demonstrate to connect the known details of the printing process with the forms of the inked shapes to be interpreted. This relationship is highly variable and, indeed, seldom so demonstrable as the more general conclusions of the analytical bibliographer.

Since it is so very pertinent here I cite once more the admirable example of Dr. Alice Walker's recovery of the exact manuscript spelling of a word in *Romeo and Juliet* Q2. At IV. i. 83 an arrangement of types spells out the word *c h a p e l s*, which in context makes no sense. A little thought shows that *chapless* is the correct reading. According to the usual deductive way of thinking it would seem likely, at first, that mechanical transposition caused the error, a fault to which compositors (like typists) are especially prone. But Dr. Walker very acutely noticed that the compositor setting this passage habitually spelled his *-ess* endings at length as

-esse, and hence would not have set the word in the truncated sequence *chaples* (distorted by inadvertent transposition to *chapels*). It followed, by induction, that the error was not mechanical but instead the result of a misreading of the manuscript. The compositor from the start had thought the word was *chapels*, and he set that sequence of types intentionally. Such a misreading could not have been made if the manuscript form of *chapless* had been spelled *-esse* (the compositor's own spelling) and very likely not as *-ess*. Hence, for this specific compositor to have made this particular error, the manuscript spelling must have been *chaples*.[1]

As opposed to this high degree of probability in establishing by the methods of textual bibliography the relationship of the printed to the manuscript form of a word, one may cite the recent controversy aroused by Dr. Hotson's attempt, using arguments from possible meanings, to identify the manuscript form with the printed *table* and thus to unsettle the classic Theobald emendation 'a babbl'd of green fields' in *Henry V*. The manuscript form cannot be recovered with any degree of certainty, for no bibliographical relationship between it and the printed form can be established in sufficient detail to be useful, one way or the other. At the most, one can appeal in support of Theobald to palaeographical possibility (a far cry indeed from bibliographical certainty), but even this weak reed is suspect, for as Greg long ago remarked, the emendation *talkd* is palaeographically closer to *table* than is *babld*. I have every confidence in *babbl'd*, but

---

[1] 'Compositor Determination and Other Problems in Shakespearian Texts', *Studies in Bibliography*, vii (1955), 9–10. One should notice the bibliographical cast of the argument, which rests entirely on the determination of a specific compositor's habitual spelling characteristics. Dr. Walker gives some other examples (p. 10): 'Similarly, Compositor A's error of "Naples" (for "napless") in *Coriolanus*, II. i. 224, would probably not have occurred if the manuscript had had the long spelling. The error is best explained as due to the misinterpretation of a manuscript short spelling, which (if Jaggard A had understood it) would have appeared in the Folio as "naplesse". Again, if we accept the Folio correction of Q1's "that accord" to "it action" in *Titus Andronicus*, v. ii. 18, we must postulate that the quarto compositor misinterpreted "yt" (for "it") as the contraction.'

I accept it as an act of faith and not because the emendation has been 'scientifically' demonstrated.

To proceed to a more complex example, we may take it that no power on earth can demonstrate bibliographically that in *Hamlet* the shared F and Q2 reading *pious bonds* is wrong, that the manuscript from which Q2 was set read *bauds*, and that in this specific reading the Folio has merely repeated a Q2 error through scribal failure to annotate the example of Q2 used as Folio printer's copy. The hypothesis that the Folio text is essentially derivative in its relationship to Q2 can apply only to show that the conditions are appropriate for an error of this sort to occur, whereas conditions would be much less appropriate if another relationship existed between the texts. Given the hypothesis for favourable conditions, common experience would then lead us to expect a certain number of such errors in the *Hamlet* text. Yet if *pious bauds* is right, the argument for it must rest almost exclusively on meaning, a literary matter. The bibliographical findings about the relationship of the texts as a whole have no more immediate application to this specific reading than to hundreds and hundreds of other shared readings that have never been questioned. All that bibliographical reasoning can do here is to admit *possibility*, a very different matter from establishing *probability*. Despite what may be a bibliographically demonstrable relationship between the two texts as a whole, no equally demonstrable relationship can be established between this specific shared word in Q2 and in the Folio. Given the partially derivative nature of the Folio text, the bibliographical evidence has no application to a decision between *bonds* and *bauds* except that *bauds* is not impossible in view of the overall governing conditions. The most that can be said in fact, is that if one plumps for *bauds* on critical evidence that is not physically inherent in the text, then bibliographical reasoning can provide a satisfactory explanation for the appearance in the Folio of an error initiated by Q2.

This bibliographical after-the-event interpretation of the Folio error is a blessing not to be ignored, as we may see from the difficulties that face editors of *2 Henry IV* who believe in the independence of the copy for the Quarto and Folio texts and so must explain away the various common errors that are present. But the bibliographical explanation is strictly inferential as applied to *bonds–bauds* in *Hamlet*, and its use should not disguise the basic fact that the case for emendation to *bauds* is of essentially the same nature as the case for Theobald's *babbl'd* in *Henry V*. Bibliographical analysis has by no means explained the original error in *Hamlet* Q2 (corresponding to *table*): if it can establish the general reliance of F on Q2 as copy, it has only made possible the nullification (if need be) of the force of the Folio's sharing of the *bonds* form. In other words, bibliographical method has established certain wide limits here in which the literary argument can be pursued instead of confining the argument to the relatively narrow logical conditions that would hold if the Folio were set throughout from manuscript.[1]

To sum up, any evidence in favour of *bauds* is mainly critical, not bibliographical. Bibliographical investigation can show that the physical conditions are such as to permit common error in Q2 and F more readily under the relationship it has determined exists between the two documents (derivation) than under another relationship (independence) that it can show does not exist. But it can never demonstrate that the manuscript used to annotate Q2 as printer's copy for

---

[1] This point is clearly seen by Professor Harold Jenkins in his arguments for still another shared error (*Modern Language Review*, liv [1959], 393–5). This is Laertes' *didst* in *Hamlet*, IV. vii. 58. In support of the proposed emendation to *diest*, Professor Jenkins remarks first that the accepted relationship of F to Q2 permits corruption originating in Q2 to be passed on to F. The point of *didst* is not clear and at best is weak. *Diest* makes especially appropriate sense in context and is palaeographically probable. Finally, most pertinent of all, the Q1 reading 'thus he dies' suggests that Q2 is corrupt. A scrupulous regard is paid to the mere permissive nature of the bibliographical conditions, and the force of the argument is applied elsewhere. All the same, the emendation might never have been proposed if the bibliographical conditions had not been favourable.

the Folio read *bauds* and that the scribe overlooked the variant.

IV. *Bibliographical Checks on Criticism*

Yet it is wrong to confine the application of textual bibliography and its laws too straitly to the establishment of any single reading, when its most valuable function is, instead, the determination of the exact conditions under which a text has been presented in print. Particular problems can then be attacked, more systematically, in accord with a general working hypothesis that accounts for their origin. None the less, the admittedly narrow points that have occupied our examination may serve to remind us that there are different orders of bibliographical evidence; and just so the function of bibliography in textual criticism is by no means limited strictly to the resolution of textual cruxes. Indeed, one of the most important applications of bibliographical method to textual criticism is to determine such large questions as the genetic relationship of texts, and thereby to establish logical requirements for the testing of purely critical solutions to the problem of the individual reading. Occurrences in which bibliographical analysis can supply the whole answer to textual cruxes are fairly limited. For every example like *shortly* versus *thereby* in *Hamlet*, or *sullied* versus *solid flesh*, where an immediate bibliographical basis for decision can exist, there are hundreds that can rely only on the general guidance of bibliographical findings that have established the derivation and relationship of the texts as a whole.

Some very important textual decisions can be made by the critic in *King Lear*, for instance, because Sir Walter Greg demonstrated from the physical evidence of press-variant quarto formes that the Folio text was set from an annotated copy of the Quarto, and not throughout from an independent manuscript. Modern editors of such plays as *King Lear*, *Othello*, and *Troilus and Cressida* have been able to make use of the newly established bibliographical relationship of Folio to Quarto as a prime logical guide in the eclectic choice of readings from the two texts. Indeed, it is not too much to assert that this critical recognition of the bibliographical limitation on conjecture, and the putting of this guidance to constructive, positive use, is a dominant motif in the new look in editorial methods since the war.[1] The exact details bearing on the physical dependence of one substantive edition upon another, as in the Shakespearian Folio–Quarto problems, are no longer matter only for the 'curious' but instead dwell at the very heart of the editorial problem. As is shown by post-war Shakespeare editions, and the remarkable interest of the reviewers—even of school and popular texts— in discussing the details of the editor's grappling with the new theories, a heightened consciousness is now in existence about the real complexity of Shakespearian textual matters. This is a healthy sign, for the criticism has been informed and intelligent, by and large, and cannot fail to leave its mark on the work of the future. And in so far as the attention has been drawn away in some part from the isolation of familiar cruxes and to a recognition of the many, many smaller readings (usually submerged) in which grounds for a choice, other than tradition, must be sought, the minute new critical consciousness has undoubtedly reflected the first effects of the bibliographical analysis of the larger problems of text.

In another direction, an editor of *Richard III* can determine the exact amount of compositorial corruption in two large sections of the Folio text and can return to the comparative purity of the Q1 readings because these lines have been established bibliographically as set from the pages of the Third Quarto and, critically, as set from unannotated pages in contrast to the rest of the Folio text for this play. In *Hamlet* Q2 an editor can almost automatically disregard the

---

[1] In this matter, as in so many others, Sir Walter Greg in pre-war years showed the way. However, it was in large part the post-war development of bibliographical methods for determining these relationships with a certainty missing before that encouraged editors to accept the real necessity to explore the textual consequences in detail.

possibility that readings in sheets E and G (and part of H) could have been contaminated by reference to the bad-quarto first edition, because analytical bibliography can show that a second compositor was setting these sheets simultaneously with the first compositor's setting of B, C, and D and what seems to have been the only copy of Q1 available was in almost constant use for consultation by the first compositor.

In some of these cases the general bibliographical determination can be applied to specific textual readings in an authoritative manner. But in most, the proper function of bibliography is to set up logical safeguards against unprincipled critical speculation and to require that critical judgement conforms to certain prerequisite conditions.

In this situation it is proper to point out that in its turn a limitation is placed on bibliographical reasoning not to interfere beyond its authority with the appropriate exercise of the critical judgement. This is a danger not usually contemplated, but it is a real one if bibliographical method is strained beyond its capacity for making authoritative decisions. The relation between the bibliographical and the critical interpretation of textual phenomena is an ever-shifting one according to widely variable circumstances. No absolute claims independent of these circumstances can be made for the pre-eminence of either discipline. If, then, critics are to consult the bibliographer when he can contribute an ostensible explanation for textual phenomena, either in general or in particular, the different degrees of certainty in bibliographical answers must not be obscured by excessive claims. All bibliographical evidence is not susceptible of equally factual interpretation. It is necessary, then, to look with some minuteness into the nature of bibliographical evidence and the variable order of certainty that can be attached to interpretations that stem from it.

NOTES

Note A, p. 39. The small number (two) of known corrections in inner C might suggest the possibility that a lost earlier stage of press-correction had existed. But if this possibility is to be taken seriously, then the few known press-corrections in outer B, inner D, and outer G, which have one, one, and two alterations respectively, must also be conjectured as second thoughts. On the other hand, it might be argued just as readily that outer N with its large number of corrections is the anomalous forme, and the other four variant formes, with no more than two corrections each, represent the normal. Some support could be adduced, indeed, from the fact pointed out by Professor Wilson that the corrections in outer N cluster in the Osric scene, which might well have caused a rise in compositorial error. Thus a conservative analysis of the evidence preserved in the variant formes suggests the danger of using outer N as a typical example of proof-reading in the quarto. If so, the hypothesis is not a compelling one that the preserved variants of inner C represent a second round, and thus that it would have been possible for other words in the forme to have been altered in a lost state. It is interesting to observe that the known variants in Q2 concern substantive alteration in the main, with only a few spelling changes. Thus it might be argued, if one were reckoning possibilities, that in the four formes the small number of variants that in other circumstances might lead one to suspect afterthoughts, in this quarto merely represent the normal original correction by a proof-reader who was generally indifferent to the correction of the accidentals.

Note B, p. 40. That pseudo-bibliographical speculation still has its charms is indicated in A. S. Cairncross, 'The Tempest, iii. i. 15, and Romeo and Juliet, i. i. 121–128', Shakespeare Quarterly, vii (1956), 448–9. Dr. Cairncross agrees with Dover Wilson's agreement with Spedding that the famous crux 'most busy lest, when I do it' at iii. i. 15 of The Tempest should read, 'most busiest when idlest.' On critical grounds this is perhaps the best emendation proposed, but regrettably he attempts to provide a bibliographical respectability for the emendation by the following 'mechanical explanation': 'The mechanical explanation seems to be that one or more letters worked loose in the forme, or more probably fell out of the compositor's stick, particularly the 'l' of 'idlest', or perhaps 'le', leaving 'id est' or 'id st', or eventually 'id t'. They were due to be replaced in front of a final 'st', and the compositor mistook the place, and restored them before the 'st' of 'busiest', where, since all the letters of the line could move to the right, there may have been a gap. The remaining letters of 'idlest' were then restored to some sort of sense either by the compositor, or more likely, by the proof-reader, in a manner familiar to all students of the First Folio text.'

The new Arden edition reprints this 'mechanical explanation' with solemnity and thereby may give it currency among the ingenuous. There is no need to suggest that the triple error necessary to account for the distortion of a hypothetically correct original setting is not restoration in a manner familiar to Dr. Hinman, the closest student of the First Folio we are likely to have. The real point of objection is more serious: the 'mechanical explanation' is not truly mechanical, or bibliographical, because it is founded on no bibliographical evidence. Nothing in the preserved typesetting of the Folio line indicates that the type was originally set correctly and then was accidentally disturbed, whether repaired properly or improperly. For all any bibliographer knows, this present form was the original typesetting. Thus if we allow such guessing-games about what a compositor might have done in repairing a quite hypo-thetical accident to become a part of textual scholarship, and treat them as 'bibliographical', we can explain most Shakespeare cruxes as we please. And two critics might easily suggest two different original readings to the same crux, depending upon which way they ingeniously preferred to think that hypo-thetically displaced or dropped-out type was repaired. If it were not for the spurious 'bibliographical' basis for such suggestions, they would be readily recognized by anyone for the idle speculation they truly represent, of no scholarly validity whatever.

Note C, p. 45. Any other view would encounter difficulties. That is, *if* F *Hamlet* were set from manuscript a very devious line of speculation would be required to attack the hypothesis that *shortly* was the manuscript reading faithfully transferred to print. On the other hand, if F were set from annotated Q2, one might speculate that the uncorrected state with *thirtie* was the copy, that the annotator overlooked the nonsense word when he was altering Q2 readings divergent from his manuscript, and that the F compositor rationalized *thirtie* into *shortly* on his own initiative. This chain of guess-work *might* be right, but no positive evidence can be found to suggest that it is. The whole case could be dismissed instantly, indeed, (*a*) if F could be shown to have been set from manuscript, or (*b*) if Q2 were the basic copy, but it could be shown that the corrected state of the forme was in the actual quarto annotated for Jaggard's compositors. In the latter event the only refuge would be that *shortly* was the F compositor's memorial error for *thereby*. But how much simpler it would be, in default of any evidence to the contrary, to assume that *shortly* was the reading in the manuscript behind F, and that—regardless of copy—it got transferred accurately to print.

Note D, p. 47. But critics and editors of the eighteenth-century literature still make one despair occasionally when they exhibit a bland disregard for the intensive research and the clarified principles that have been characteristic of scholarship devoted to the editorial problems of the sixteenth and seventeenth centuries. Greg's classic set of principles in 'The Rationale of Copy-Text', *Studies in Bibliography*, iii (1951), 19–36, was written in vain if critics will pay no more attention to it than David Daiches, who, reviewing *The Poems of Robert Fergusson* (*Modern Language Review*, liv [1959], 262), remarks approv-ingly 'Mr. McDiarmid has very properly adopted the principle laid down by

Bruce Dickins in his 1925 edition of the Scots poems, that "the latest print which the author could possibly have overseen" should be preferred, and he has therefore reproduced the text of the 1773 *Poems*'. With some conservatism it may be said that Greg in 1951 has outmoded Dickins in 1925, and the event ought to have been recognized by so excellent a critic in 1959.

A side remark of mine in *Textual and Literary Criticism* that, in editing, the eighteenth century is 'a field that has usually been one of the disgraces of scholarship' has not received universal approbation. But without bibliographical preparation there can be little good editing, and for the state of bibliographical affairs that concern text in this period, W. B. Todd's *New Adventures Among Old Books: An Essay in Eighteenth Century Bibliography* (University of Kansas Publications, Library Series no. 4, 1958) makes alarming reading. Dr. Todd takes as typical the great Rothschild collection, catalogued in 1954, and shows how many supposed first editions are no such thing, and how many more are suspect. Even so, in this renowned collection, 'with few exceptions, what we know of all the books just mentioned is represented in the casual essays of several persons not as yet engaged in the systematic study of any one author. These are accidental discoveries, some in the work of authors not closely examined in the last twenty years, some of authors who have never been examined at all' (pp. 8–9). Even the basic bibliographical reference books are lacking for the eighteenth century: 'For 15th century English books there are at least six standard references, all under continuous revision and reclassification, for the 16th century three or four comprehensive accounts, for the 17th century two or three, for the 18th century not a one. Such is the lamentable state of affairs' (p. 10). After further analysis of the state of bibliography and some chilling examples of the complexities of the publication of a few selected literary texts, Dr. Todd concludes, 'Thus we go on preparing catalogues of what we think are first editions, publishing reprints of what we believe to be the authoritative text, and uttering opinions on what we suppose are the final statements of our authors, all in ignorance of evidence which, some time, may require that we do everything over again' (p. 33). Dr. Todd has an exceptionally close acquaintance with the investigation and ordering of eighteenth-century editions, and we may not suppose that he has exaggerated the seriousness of the situation. Certainly his essay offers no grounds for complacency.

Note E, p. 50. Some of the bibliographical results of this type-analysis were illustrated in C. J. K. Hinman, 'Cast-Off Copy for the First Folio of Shakespeare', *Shakespeare Quarterly*, vi (1955), 259–73. The only application to the identification of the compositors that has been published in a journal is his 'The Prentice Hand in the Tragedies of the Shakespeare First Folio: Compositor E', *Studies in Bibliography*, ix (1957), 3–20. The distinction of A, C, and D appears in Dr. Hinman's monograph on the printing of the Folio (Clarendon Press, 1963).

The increasing complexity of textual bibliography is coming to require a textual critic to be a practising analytical bibliographer as well, so that he can himself make the technical analysis of text. This is a strictly modern development that will have far-reaching results in the future. Certainly it means that advanced analytical bibliography, especially in its textual application, will need to be a subject for formal instruction in graduate studies.

III

THE INTERPRETATION OF EVIDENCE: THE DEMONSTRABLE AND PROBABLE

1. *The Demonstrable and Probable in Interpretation*

THE interpretation of bibliographical evidence is a necessary step following on the identification of the tangible material capable of serving as this evidence. Since not all physical evidence can be interpreted with equal authority, the textual critic needs to discriminate between the concrete details from which relatively certain conclusions can be drawn and those that at best can be only suggestive. In this matter what I may term the 'postulate of normality' is important in the theory of bibliographical investigation bearing on textual problems. One will often find, for example, that the available bibliographical evidence would lead to a demonstrable interpretation provided only that, without qualification, one could assume normality in the printing process.

Although printing is a mechanical operation, its tools and machines are managed by human beings, not by robots. The actions of these men engaged in a routine mechanical process can be recovered, and thereafter forecast, in general with some accuracy. It is true that the unpredictable in any individual can always pop up. Human forgetfulness may cause a workman to blunder; memorial lapses may produce strange consequences. McKerrow, as I recall, once remarked that some contradictory pieces of evidence could be reconciled most easily by the hypothesis that the entire printing-house had adjourned to the nearest pub and got drunk. None the less, tempting as this or similar jocularities might be to the harried bibliographer, no one should base a theory on abnormality instead of on normality of individual routine operation unless there is overwhelming evidence in favour of the aberration. If we were allowed only on a deductive basis to postulate individual error, no laws of bibliographical evidence could exist, for the unknown human equation could successfully 'explain' any abnormality observed.

Normality must be considered first as it may apply to the routine practices or customs of the printing trade, and, second, to the routine details with which a workman would carry out these trade operations.

An example of the routine practice of the trade would be the transfer of lines of type from the stick directly into the Elizabethan page galley instead of the long or slip galley of later times. This procedure has been reconstructed on sound evidence, and exceptions have not been observed. Here it seems manifestly true that individual shop and general trade operation coincided exactly. On the other hand, a trade custom mentioned in early printing descriptions consisted in placing the inner forme first on the press. Often there are mechanical reasons why this order is advisable,[1] and it would appear that in some shops the tradition persisted whether or not the mechanical causes for it were operative in any individual book. Other shops, however, sent the formes to press in more or less random order when both formes of a sheet had been composed prior to imposition; and therefore we cannot assume in any given shop the priority of the inner forme, as a normal postulate, without very precise evidence. 'Normality' in the printing-house, then, could consist in the invariable use of page galleys, but often in no fixed order of the formes through the press. In the one, we need no longer secure specific evidence to assure ourselves that any seventeenth-century book under examination was set directly into pages.

[1] If the pages of a sheet are set in seriatim order, the last page of the inner forme will be completed before the last page of the outer forme can be composed. Thus if the press is waiting, the compositor will impose and give to the pressman the earliest forme possible, which will be the inner. Thereafter, if an equal balance exists between printing and composing time, the inner forme will always be sent to the press before the outer in order to prevent delay.

In the other, we can never make any fixed assumptions and must decide for any given book only on specific evidence.

It is a reasonable assumption that a workman performing a mechanical task will conform to the traditional means that have been found efficient for the job in hand. For instance, it is most unlikely, and there is no evidence to suggest, that a given helper at the press who put the paper on the pins would ignore the routine turning of the heap for perfecting in favour of his twirling each sheet by hand. We may not believe that a given compositor would suddenly become bored with the standard imposition of type-pages in quarto, say, and would introduce a variant imposition requiring the sheet to be turned not end for end to perfect, but instead sideways on the long axis. When a compositor had accumulated as many lines of type in his stick as made it too heavy to continue comfortably, he would transfer the type to the page galley that was being filled: we can assume readily enough that he would not regularly transfer the type line by line as each was set.

On the other hand, some option might exist that would result in slight variation in the routine performance of details. A compositor might fall into a general routine, say in quarto printing, of distributing his type after setting sig. 2^v of a gathering; but if his cases remained sufficiently full of the types he was utilizing, he might well stretch the usual period between distributions in any sheet to $3 or 3^v, just as if he became short of types, he might narrow the interval and distribute at $2. In another situation, if the nature of the copy led to a run on certain letters, he might choose to distribute earlier than usual in order to secure the needed sorts, or at his option he might get along by using roman for depleted italic letters, say, until it was convenient to re-supply his cases by distribution. If he were well ahead of the press, he might choose to impose his inner forme on completion and only then continue and set the last page of the outer forme, or at his option he might set that page and then make his imposition. In this process he might routinely first impose the inner to send to the press, or, indifferently, he might impose the outer forme. We must learn to distinguish clearly between the anticipated 'normal' routine performance of the details of the operation and those in which an option was demonstrably 'normal' and no entirely fixed and invariable set of motions was enforced on a workman.

It is a violation of the postulate of normality to conjecture without the full backing of specific evidence that a routine, whether of trade, shop, or man, established as consistent in its nature and practice, has been violated to produce results that seem bibliographically anomalous. As D. F. Foxon puts it:

Printing, like other crafts, is at once efficient and intensely conservative; the materials and tools changed little between 1500 and 1800, and there was little if any increase in the speed of work for the reason that highly efficient methods were already established at an early time. Since there was a traditional method of doing everything, we should never put forward an argument which assumes an abnormal method of work without producing good evidence for that method having been followed and a reason why the usual method was rejected.[1]

This is a distinction that needs repeating and repeating, Common experience shows the frequency of human error within the confines of a routine operation when the full intention was to carry out the routine. A compositor's fingers may outrun his memory and he may easily transpose two letters in a word, or two words in relation to each other. A startlingly common textual error is the transposition of punctuation, by memorial failure or anticipation, between the caesura and the end of a line of verse, or between the ends of two consecutive lines, or even between the end of one verse and the caesura of the next. This is unconscious error within normal operations. But it is a very different matter from the assumption of the kind of error that rests on deducing an abnormal departure from routine. For instance, in an article recently submitted by a student to *Studies in Bibliography*, a

[1] *The Technique of Bibliography* (The Book, no. 6, 1955), p. 16.

complexly formed and unusual gathering—almost certainly
the result of cancellation and substitution—was explained as
the result of an imposition of the type-pages that has never
existed for the format and would require special folding. No
reason was offered why normality had been violated: the
student's inexperience led him to believe, falsely, that if he
could deduce some manner of imposition that could create
the anomalies in the gathering, he had offered a satisfactory
bibliographical explanation.

One textual critic of my acquaintance, in the latter hours
of an evening is fond of producing a private speculation for
the existence of some extremely odd misplacement of speech-
prefixes that now and then occur in Elizabethan plays.
These, he says, could be explained if the compositor set
speech-prefixes the way a scribe may copy them, that is, as
an independent operation after the full page of the text had
been completed. In such circumstances his eye might catch
the wrong line when he returned to the text to insert the
characters' names before their speeches.

The analogy with what seems to have been the practice of
some theatrical scribes is inexact because the conditions are
so different as to make such a procedure impossible for the
compositor. The scribe wrote a full line of dialogue that required the speech-prefixes to be inserted in the left margin.
The usual printing practice was to indent the prefix. Hence
the line of type containing a speech-prefix could not be justified until the prefix was set and inserted, and to justify a line
in page galley instead of in the composing stick would be
a nuisance and seemingly a more difficult operation without
the uniform measure provided by the stick. Given this
mechanical difficulty, one may query what comparable gain
would accrue to the compositor in the mass setting of prefixes save for the slight convenience that the italic type would
all come from the one case, though from a case not convenient to the place where the page galley was resting.

But all this is argument from possibility, from a deductive

theory of what might be the simplest way of performing a printing operation. Positive bibliographical evidence, fortunately, is available to demonstrate inductively that, in some plays at least, the prefixes were set quite normally before proceeding to the first line of the speech. When the italic letters ran low in the case owing to an unusual drain, compositors were in the habit of substituting roman for the depleted italic sorts. Every time that I have seen this substitution in the italic of the speech-prefixes, the same substitution has appeared in the italic within the text. Moreover, if part of the way down a page the compositor paused to distribute and so secured an adequate supply of type for the remainder, the substitution ceases simultaneously in prefix and in text. This is positive proof in favour of 'normal' setting of speech-prefixes in dramatic printing and it derives from evidence collateral to that which must be explained. And once the usual method has been established in this manner, it is impossible to continue to deduce only from the evidence of the anomalous prefixes that the errors resulted from mass setting. Some different cause must be sought, such as errors in the manuscript, misreading of the manuscript, or memorial failure. These are normal conjectures, for they envisage inadvertencies within the established routine.

On the contrary, to posit a kind of error that would come from a departure from standard routine, one would need such supplementary evidence as a clash between the signs of type-shortage in the prefixes and in the text. Definite evidence other than the aberration itself that is to be explained must be required if a theory is to hold for the occurrence of error through non-routine operation.

As another example, routine typesetting produces occasional transposed words. When, except for the neutral evidence of the transposition itself, there is no sign that anything other than memorial failure occurred, it is improper, and quite useless, to build up an elaborate theory of an omitted word caught by the proof-reader and marked in the margin, but inserted by the compositor in the wrong place, or some other romance for which no collateral evidence exists. In a sense this argument for normality is a form of the argument for simplicity of which Sir Walter Greg was so fond. The appeal to normality does, ordinarily, explain a difficulty in the simplest manner.

In my own limited experience, the evidence of press-corrections indicates that the white-paper formes in a heap were generally perfected in the exact order of their original printing.[1] However, in at least one preserved copy of sheet F of Dekker's *Match Me in London* (1631) the variants show that this routine operation was an impossibility. One can easily deduce a variation of process or of handling that would produce this one seemingly irregular sheet. We might speculate, for instance, that in some unknown way a sheet got misplaced. Or we might guess that not one but several proof sheets had been given to the corrector; and when the extra proofs were returned to the heap, perfecting had advanced to the point where the anomaly would be produced since the variant type in one forme would then be out of phase with the variant impression in the proof-forme. Some irregularity in the handling of the details of the routine operation could be made out to be plausible enough. But we should not permit ourselves to advance such an explanation without supplementary evidence.

The difficulty is this. To demonstrate an isolated aberration in routine operations is almost impossible; hence only the exhaustion of human ingenuity could set a limit to conjectures that might quite plausibly be made if the principle of individual variation were accepted as a satisfactory manner of explaining abnormal evidence. Moreover, common biblio-graphical experience shows ultimately that most of these

---

[1] Dr. Hinman has had a contrary experience in analysing the practice of the Shakespeare First Folio, I hasten to add. Here the variants do not necessarily back each other in a regular manner. Whether this is a special characteristic of Jaggard's shop at the time I do not know.

unique explanations based on human failure or unpredictable variation of routine handling are wrong. Indeed, if explanations are continually sought within the normal operation, the truth will usually be discovered. In the specific example of *Match Me in London* and its sheet that was perfected out of phase, an insistence on explaining the anomaly in normal terms led to the hypothesis that the heap was not always turned all at once before perfecting was begun, and that some number of the sheets might not always be turned until perfecting was well advanced. This hypothesis could scarcely be examined more closely in the one example, but fortunately Dr. Hinman is able to show from abundant evidence that various First Folio sheets have exactly the same characteristics and must have been produced under similar conditions.

11. *The Postulate of Normality and Scientific Method*

The bibliographer must always start with the postulate of normality. However, the human equation with all its unpredictability is not completely disbarred from this postulate. Compositors' fingers will not always correctly translate the impulses of their brains, and so transpositions, repetitions, omissions, and the like will occur in typesetting as well as such mechanical aberrations as foul-case. Certain printing processes must necessarily allow within limits for normal variation. But otherwise we must throw out the human equation as much as we can in our search to find an explanation for seeming aberrancies.[1] Instead, these apparent irregularities should force us to reconsider our ideas about the permissible variations in the printer's routine, and often— in the course of this salutary process of reconsideration—we may come upon the truth.[2] Only at the price of this limiting of speculation can analytical bibliography (including its

---

[1] See note A, p. 95.

[2] This is one of the justifications for pure bibliographical research without direct literary connexion in its primary objectives. See 'Some Relations of Bibliography to Editorial Problems', *Studies in Bibliography*, iii (1950), 38–43.

derivative, textual bibliography) associate itself with scientific method as it must endeavour to do. In so far as bibliography can produce invariable results from controlled experiment, it can approach the scientific in its discipline and its results. This supreme virtue is destroyed if seeming contradictions are interpreted as the product of unique aberration within the mechanical process.

Moreover, the postulate of normality depends on the working hypothesis that all that we know at any given time must be the truth, and therefore the details of the printing process and their handling that have been recovered (when tolerably full) must represent 'normality' unless we have stubbornly inexplicable evidence to the contrary. This hypothesis is necessary in some part because a confirmation of the validity of inductive bibliographical reasoning is that it leads us, by a series of tests of the evidence, to an explanation consistent with our knowledge of normality. (A different matter, incidentally, from deducing an explanation of evidence from this knowledge of normality.) Also, since certainty about every small detail in the operation is difficult to attain, it is essential whenever we can to assume that we know the general process of printing, for otherwise conjecture from evidence would be paralysed for lack of some standard for confirmation, or would have no bounds set to mere guesswork. Doubtless it was possible for the Elizabethans to print in many more ways than those we have recovered; but if our concepts of 'normality' are to be challenged, the conviction of error will not be made by guesses of 'what might have been' to explain the apparently abnormal evidence of a single book, or often of a single reading.

No one can argue that we know all about the printing processes of the past, and it is just as obvious that from time to time this postulate of normality has fostered incorrect explanations based on imperfect evidence. But the principle gives us something to build on and offers some procedures for testing the interpretation of evidence. An alert bibliographer may thereby extend or correct our understanding of normality by new interpretations of evidence confirmed either on internal grounds in a wholly different manner or else by similar evidence in other books, the significance of which is now seen in a new light.

For instance, it has been a useful principle, and one that has retained a substantial part of its truth under modification, that in the normal process of proof-reading and correcting a book printed with two skeleton-formes to the sheet, an invariant forme backing a variant forme contains type that has already been read and corrected.[1] We now know that the seriatim setting of type-pages is not the only 'normal' method, and we must henceforth include as part of 'normality' the setting of pages out of seriatim order and by formes from cast-off copy. This setting by formes is found invariably in the First Folio, and investigators have discovered it also in enough dramatic quartos to suggest that it may have been a common printing practice.[2]

As a consequence, what has been the usual interpretation of the proof-reading of two-skeleton books is true only for the seriatim setting of type-pages and would often be false for pages that had been set by formes.[3] We knew an appreciable

[1] See 'Elizabethan Proofing', *Joseph Quincy Adams Memorial Studies* (1948), pp. 571–86.

[2] See, for instance, John H. Smith, 'The Composition of the Quarto of *Much Ado About Nothing*', *Studies in Bibliography*, xvi (1963), 9–26, and citations in footnote 7, to which should be added Robert K. Turner, 'Printing Methods and Textual Problems in *A Midsummer Night's Dream* Q1', ibid. (1962), xv 33–55, and John Russell Brown, 'The Printing of John Webster's Plays', ibid., pp. 57–69. The basic study is George Walton Williams, 'Setting by Formes in Quarto Printing', ibid. xi (1958), 39–53.

[3] Since copy would usually be set by formes unless a correct ratio of compositor to press could be obtained, it follows that under most circumstances the second forme would not be composed by the time the first was ready for correction of the type. In seriatim setting only one page needs setting beyond the inner forme to complete the outer, whereas in setting by formes the whole second forme needs doing. Thus the pause in press-work while the first forme is being corrected after the initial early reading could not ordinarily be filled by putting the second forme on the press to secure proofs.

part of the truth from our earlier understanding of 'normality' as applied to the process of proof-reading. But we now know a great deal more under our extended concept. Although experience now shows that some hypotheses based on the assumption of seriatim setting were wrong in books set by formes, yet this is no argument against the observance of the postulate. Without it, little confidence could have been felt in the interpretation of the evidence in the numerous books that our later and better information shows to have been quite correct.

Scientific method builds on what it knows, step by step, disregarding wrong hypotheses when their bases are shown to be insufficiently factual. That the working hypotheses of physics are occasionally modified in various serious respects does not mean that physics as a science, and its method, should be replaced by unmethodical speculation. So with bibliography. New discoveries extend our knowledge, modify our concepts but seldom show that everything that has been believed is dead wrong. Thus bibliography joins with science in requiring the assumption of normality as the basis for any working hypothesis. Any working hypothesis, in turn, is taken as leading only to provisional truth, but a truth strong enough to serve as the basis for critical decision. When a hypothesis will no longer work, then we are automatically forced to a more comprehensive and extended working hypothesis, and our understanding of truth is enlarged, even though only provisionally, and our scholarly techniques are refined.

III. *Evidence in Relation to the Postulate*

The postulate of normality works best when sufficient evidence is present from which to reason and the chief use of the postulate is to serve as a check on the interpretation of the evidence and not, in a sense, as part of the evidence itself or its interpretation. It may work fairly well in a few special cases when some evidence is present bearing on the matter but not enough to sustain demonstration. Even though an appeal from time to time will prove faulty, the odds may be said to favour 'normality' under controlled conditions. If one collates 20 copies of a book and finds in sheet B that only 1 copy shows the uncorrected state of the type as against 19 showing the corrected, 'normality' makes it highly probable that the correction in B was made at an earlier point in time in the machining of this forme than the correction of a forme in C that shows 19 with uncorrected type and only 1 with corrected. Despite the fact that statistics can lie, the mathematical odds are excellent that this sampling of 20 copies can be extrapolated in accord with normality.

On the other hand, evidence that by its nature is neutral, and thus wholly dependent upon interpretation for significance, may be used in an appeal to normality only with the utmost caution and seldom in an effort to prove a higher degree than simple possibility. If a critical doubt exists about which is the uncorrected and which the corrected state of a press-variant forme, as will sometimes happen, experience will suggest the normal possibility that the state with the fewer extant copies is the earlier. But this appeal to 'normality' is treacherous. In the first place, the possibility exists that the extant copies (when few) do not accurately represent the original proportion of states in the full edition-sheet. Of much more moment, however, is this warning: whereas it is often found that press-correction in a forme as part of the normal proof-reading process will take place at a relatively early time in its printing, this early correction is by no means so 'normal' as to carry a great deal of weight in any specific instance without corroborative evidence.

Certainly, statistics will favour early correction as a general proposition. In Dekker's *Patient Grissel* (1603) some sheets are 3 to 1 in favour of the corrected states; in his *Satiromastix* (1602), a rough average would be about 14 to 3; in *Westward Ho* (1607) about 14 to 3; in *2 Honest Whore* (1630) about 14 to 3. But in *Patient Grissel* forme C(i) has

only a single corrected state to 3 uncorrected in the four
extant copies; in *Satiromastix* E(i) and M(o) have only 9
corrected to 8 uncorrected states, and M(i) has 5 corrected to
12 uncorrected, though this may represent a special case. In
Westward Ho, although four formes run as high as 16
corrected to 1 uncorrected, A(o) has only 9 corrected to 7
uncorrected.[1] Instances of proof-correction relatively late in
the run are not uncommon, even though most formes were
undoubtedly corrected fairly early. Consequently, if other
evidence is wanting than that of the proportion of copies
preserved in the two states, only bare possibility could
favour a decision based in any specific case on the assumed
'normality' of early proof-reading.

To try to use the postulate of normality is dangerous when
evidence is largely wanting, and pure deduction must be
made on little more than the suggestion that what evidence
there is is not inconsistent with our view of normal printing.
Such cases are usually difficult to assess, since all depends
upon the kind of evidence balanced against its extent.
Unfortunately, open or disguised appeals to normality that
are basically untenable are far too common in uninformed
bibliographical writing. One illustration must suffice. It is
true that in general the Elizabethans printed works in folio
that they considered to be of a superior merit or of some
permanent value. It is true that some of these folios were
carefully proof-read, like the Jonson 1616 Folio. But it does
not follow that, on practically no evidence, a writer can conjecture that, because of its format, Jaggard's proof-reader of
the Shakespeare First Folio and also its compositors were

---

[1] The figures for these plays are as follows: *Patient Grissel* C(i): 1(c)–3(u); D(o):
2(c)–1(u); F(i): 2(c)–1(u); G(1): 3(c)–1(u); I(i): 3(c)–1(u). *Satiromastix* B(i): 16(c)–
1(u); C(o): 15(c)–2(u); E(i): 9(c)–8(u); F(o): 16(c)–1(u); I(o): 14(c)–3(u); I(i):
14(c)–3(u); K(o): 15(c)–2(u); L(o): 11(c)–6(u); M(o): 9(c)–8(u); M(i): 5(c)–12(u).
Westward Ho A(o): 9(c)–7(u); C(o): 15(c)–2(u); D(i): 13(c)–4(u); E(o): 11(c)–
6(u); E(i): 16(c)–1(u); F(o): 16(c)–1(u); F(i): 16(c)–1(u); G(o): 16(c)–1(u); I(o):
11(c)–6(u). *2 Honest Whore* B(i): 16(c)–1(u); C(i): 15(c)–2(u); G(o); 14(c)–3(u);
H(i): 16(c)–1(u).

more ready to 'correct' errors on their own initiative than their opposite numbers in the houses that printed the Shakespeare quartos.[1] Dr. Hinman's patient assembling of the facts shows how idle is this guess. From him we learn that the proof-reading of the Folio was, indeed, particularly unconcerned with the substantive errors that had been in the first critic's mind. It is my own observation that the average Dekker quarto received more proof-reader's alteration of its readings and their forms than did the Shakespeare text in the First Folio, proportionally. So much for guess-work and for deducing from assumed normality in any specific case without proper evidence.

iv. *The Three Orders of Certainty*

The interpretation of bibliographical evidence is a necessary step following on the identification of the evidence. Since all physical evidence cannot be interpreted with equal certainty, the textual critic needs to distinguish carefully physical facts from which positive conclusions can be drawn from those that can claim only probability, and certainly from those that at best can be only suggestive, or possible.

It is convenient to assign bibliographical evidence and its interpretation to these three different orders of certainty— the demonstrable, the probable, and the possible—with the proviso that every shade can exist between the divisions, which by their nature cannot always be hard and fast.

In the first range comes physical evidence that leaves no loophole for opinion: the bibliographical case is demonstrable and admits of no controversy. A familiar example is the play *The Dumb Knight* (1608) by Gervase Markham, which has two different title-pages, with and without the author's name. Of this play Sir Edmund Chambers observed: 'The Epistle says that "Rumour hath made strange constructions on this Dumb Knight", and that "having a partner in the wrong whose worth hath been often approved . . . I now in his

[1] J. K. Walton, *The Copy for the Folio Text of Richard III* (1955), p. 19.

absence make this apology, both for him and me." Presumably these "constructions" led to the withdrawal of Markham's name from the title-page.'[1]

This interpretation illustrates the danger of literary or historical criticism attempting to operate in a field that is the bibliographer's preserve. The fallacy in method was the lack of investigation of the physical process by which the name was added or removed. When Sir Walter Greg came to this book he did not concern himself with deductions about the behaviour of authors; instead, he attacked the problem of determining, from the physical evidence, just how the two titles were printed. This inductive method quickly revealed that the title-leaf without the name is the original, firmly attached in the gathering to its conjugate leaf; and the title-leaf with the name is a cancel substitute intended to replace the original. The name has been added, therefore, and not removed. This distinction between the original and a substitute title-leaf is a physical fact that can be interpreted in a manner to settle the case in a court of law.

A similar example occurs in the quarto of *Troilus and Cressida* (1609). In early criticism the deduced order of its two title-leaves and the preface was precisely wrong. But even after the fact of cancellation and substitution was established, and the correct order settled, the inference prevailed that the cancel with the preface had been provoked by objections following on the original publication. However, the final bibliographical demonstration showed quite clearly that the cancel fold had been printed as part of the last gathering of the text and hence that it constituted a pre-publication state decided on before public sale could have offered any opportunity for objections. Conjecture about the historical reasons for the cancel must henceforth be rigidly limited by this framework of fact.[2]

[1] *Elizabethan Stage*, iii (1923), 418.
[2] Philip Williams, Jr., 'The "Second Issue" of Shakespeare's *Troilus and Cressida*, 1609', *Studies in Bibliography*, ii (1949–50), 25–33.

In the above two examples, the physical structure of a tangible object was affected by excision and substitution, and hence the demonstration of the order was absolute. Mechanical evidence may still afford demonstration, however, if the logical conclusions are such that a contrary view could be held only as mere fantasy. For instance, in the question of the misdated Pavier Quartos, it is not conceivable that anyone would argue that the false dates are in fact genuine and that the standing type used in the production of the various title-pages of different date should not be interpreted in the usual manner. One would scarcely wish to assert that this type was actually passed on from printer to printer, over the years, as a convenience. Obviously, there are dangers when we move from what are irreversible facts to appeals to an informed judgement to accept the only interpretation of evidence that seems to lie within the bounds of sanity. The question is no longer one of kind but instead of degree. Indeed, what to the wise would seem fantastic might to the ignorant appear to make quite excellent sense and to be extremely probable.[1] Moreover, no matter how rigorous the logical treatment of evidence, the factual basis for the argument may be incomplete, owing to unknown gaps in the physical evidence or to our defective knowledge of the printing process. Thus if the reasoning depends upon a concealed false premiss, quite erroneous conclusions may be reached.

v. *The Demonstrable*

Most problems, it would seem, need to be decided on their merits. However, two suggestions may be offered that will assist in settling troublesome cases. First, I should urge that the whole is greater than the sum of its parts in the evaluation of bibliographical evidence. Various pieces of evidence may exist, each of a nature that could at the very

---

[1] As in the argument for a fantastic imposition arrangement of type-pages to explain the anomalies produced in a gathering by cancellation and substitution (see pp. 67–68 above).

most suggest only a possibility; but their concurrence (especially if they are of different kinds) may rapidly tend to pyramid the strength of the total towards certainty. Secondly, I should myself exclude from this upper level of bibliographical evidence all solutions dependent upon an initial generalization about printing practices instead of upon specific evidence that such and such a method of printing was actually employed. The initial assumption may be wrong and thus provide a false premiss deriving from insufficient evidence.

A case in point occurs in the cancel fold of *Troilus and Cressida*, already remarked.[1] If, say, the evidence for the printing of the new title-leaf and the preface in the same forme as the final half-sheet of the text had rested merely on the appearance in the cancel fold of the same watermark design found in the text sheets of the quarto, the argument would fall far short of demonstration. The exact relationship of the half-sheet cancel to final half-sheet M of the text cannot be demonstrated by such evidence. No basic assumption is valid that requires similarity of paper stock to have resulted from continuous printing. The printer could have had in his shop a somewhat larger supply of this paper than was required for printing the quarto, or he could have purchased more paper (supplied by the wholesaler fortuitously from the same mill) to print the extra half-sheet, and thus the cancel fold could have been printed at a later time and still have utilized the same paper.[2]

Correspondingly, the fact that the lower half of the cancel title-page was printed from the standing type of the original will not by itself support the assumption of continuous printing. Since the title-leaf forms part of the first text gathering, the type could have been standing for about a fortnight by the time half-sheet M was printed; and there is no reason to suppose that it could not have been left undistributed for a further period if its types were not required.

[1] See note B, pp. 95–96.   [2] See note C, p. 96.

It is interesting that the printer's measure for the text of the address in the cancellans is the same as the measure in the body of the text, this suggesting that an attempt was being made to fit the type-pages of the cancel into an undistributed skeleton-forme from the same book, and possibly even into the skeletons that would have been imposed about half-sheet M. But the similarity of measure could easily be fortuitous and so without bearing on the time of manufacture.

Evidence of more significance appears when in the twelve known copies containing the cancel we find the invariable division of watermark and its absence between half-sheets ¶ and M that would suggest that the two were machined together as a full sheet and then cut apart by the binder to be placed at either end of the collated quartos. The odds are very high indeed that such concurrence in twelve copies would not be due to chance; and this evidence would certainly promote *high probability* for the hypothesis of twin half-sheet imposition of the two folds, but not absolute demonstration, perhaps, when only twelve copies are known.

However, more evidence is available. It is recognized that if running-titles from both formes of a preceding full sheet appear in both formes of a half-sheet, the pattern shows that this half-sheet must have been imposed and printed with something else by twin half-sheet arrangement. This is the pattern found in the transfer of the running-titles from sheet L to half-sheet M in *Troilus*. Alone, this evidence could not demonstrate that the something else printed with half-sheet M was the cancel fold.[1] But fortunately we can now multiply

---

[1] The pattern of running-titles would fit the printing of M as a full sheet of four leaves; but since there are only two pages of text and a blank leaf known in preserved copies, it would be fantasy to argue that the printer would print a full sheet with six blank pages rather than a half-sheet with two. Moreover, since in the copies that preserve blank M2 this leaf is conjugate with M1, a fold in the M2.3 position (or M1.4) would need to have been abstracted from all the known copies. In *Troilus* the preliminary cancel contains none of the text running-titles. If these could have been present and if they had fitted into the pattern found in half-sheet M, the solution would have come close to demonstration on such evidence alone.

the significance of the watermark evidence once the running-titles have indicated the method of imposition. And when all other evidence concurs without exception with this juncture of watermark and imposition evidence, we are justified in saying that practical demonstration has been achieved.[1] It is proper to call attention to the interlocking evidence of the running-titles and the watermarks: singly neither could have afforded more than high probability, but together they assure certainty. Moreover, in the interpretation of these two important pieces of bibliographical evidence, an appeal was not made to general expectations about printing but instead to concrete evidence pointing towards the precise method of machining together the formes of the two half-sheets. The evidence of the running-titles was the more precise, perhaps, but it was the concurrence of the evidence of the watermarks that alone could establish the actual connexion of the cancel half-sheet and M.[2]

Dr. Hinman gives me my next example. The letter 'd' in line 27 of the second column of sig. m6 of the Shakespeare First Folio was damaged during the course of printing so that some copies have the page with the undamaged and some with the damaged letter.[3] But this same piece of type that was demonstrably damaged during the printing of quire m also appears in quires d, e, f, g, and $^\chi$gg, all of these being gatherings that precede quire m in the register of the Folio. Only two conclusions can be drawn: either all the quires from d to $^\chi$gg are cancels printed later than gathering m, or else, in the normal course, gathering m preceded the

[1] The problem is worked out in detail in Philip Williams, Jr., 'The "Second Issue" of Shakespeare's *Troilus and Cressida*, 1609', *Studies in Bibliography*, ii (1949–50), 25–33.

[2] Of course, if a larger number of copies had been preserved, all of which contained the same pattern of watermarks to show beyond all statistical doubt that the two half-sheets had been cut apart from the same full sheet in copy after copy, no other evidence need have existed to prove the case. In this instance, twelve copies were not quite enough, perhaps, for absolute demonstration.

[3] See note D, pp. 96–97.

printing of these other quires. When copious evidence is available to show that the intervening gatherings are not cancels, and positive evidence for the printing of gathering m before d and the rest is also available, one can pyramid some startlingly small pieces of evidence to show the truth of a most unexpected conclusion. It is scarcely necessary to mention Dr. Hinman's quite sensational discovery, built up inductively from the physical evidence of some hundreds of damaged types, that the whole of the Folio copy was cast-off and the type-pages were set by formes in great part out of seriatim order.

vi. *The Probable*

In the second category the interpretation of the bibliographical evidence will afford only probability, not true demonstration. Here we have various subdivisions according to the nature of the evidence. A common instance of probability is one in which the bibliographical evidence might lead to an inexorable conclusion provided we could demonstrate normality in the printing process, but unfortunately only an assumption can be warranted. Or else, we may have an open choice between two known methods of printing, each of which would come under the heading of normality, but specific evidence in favour of the exact process is wanting. Or high probability may result when, in broad terms, the evidence is insufficient, or when the cumulation of a number of pieces of separately insufficient evidence into a demonstrable pattern is not possible. In most cases, if not in all, there is some specific evidence in the text that may be related to our ideas of general printing procedure, but the relationship is weak or incomplete.

When properly applied, an appeal to the postulate of normality need not automatically lower a bibliographical interpretation from the demonstrable to the probable, although every problem must be individually judged. In some bibliographical demonstrations the appeal to normality is so unnecessary as to be omitted without loss from the marshalling of evidence. For instance, we may quite comfortably believe that the conjugate form of the title-leaf in Markham's *Dumb Knight* represents the original; and the disjunct form, the substitute. We do not first need to survey, and then reject for want of evidence, the possibility that the original form is lost, that the cancellans leaf represents the second form, and that the preserved conjugate form is a third in a deliberately reprinted full sheet.

Nevertheless, (*a*) the more possible it is that alternative methods could appear within 'normality', or (*b*) the greater the need to interpret evidence deductively, owing to a lack of sufficient evidence for full inductive demonstration, then the more likely it is that the borderline between certainty and probability has been crossed.

(*a*) Let us take as our first example the possibility that alternative methods can be equally 'normal'. Ordinarily that a cancel leaf would be invariant in its form would seem to be so normal an assumption as to escape question; yet the cancel G1 in Congreve's *Double Dealer* (1694) was machined for convenience in duplicate typesettings. A textual critic can find the most desirable combination of recto and verso settings only in one perhaps aberrant fine-paper copy, although he could have reconstructed this combination even if the two pages had not existed back to back in any copy.[1] Any single leaf may be machined from one or from two or more typesettings at the printer's option. Hence the experienced critic is better off with an assumption of probability in such a case unless enough copies are available to expose duplicate setting if it had existed.[2]

---

[1] 'The Cancel Leaf in Congreve's *Double Dealer* 1694', *Papers of the Bibliographical Society of America*, xliii (1949), 78–82.

[2] One may not blandly ignore such possibilities. For example, a cancel title-leaf ordinarily exists in but one typesetting; yet George Sandys's *Christs Passion* (1640) has four, since it was found more convenient to make four typesettings of the same cancel and to impose and print them together. The single leaf that bridges the two sections, simultaneously set by two compositors, of John Crowne's *Country Wit* (1675) was set in duplicate for quicker or more convenient printing.

(*b*) The second case is one in which the need to treat evidence deductively lowers the validity of the argument from the certain to the probable. It may be, for instance, that a bibliographer can demonstrate that the first text gathering of a book was printed with the inner forme first on the press, and that a later gathering, three or four quires after, also had its inner forme first printed. Even when the regular transfer of the headlines indicates no disruption, it is better only to infer the probability that the intervening formes were printed in a similar manner, for such headline evidence, though weighty, is not infallible. Wanting other evidence, such as can be derived from the application of collimated light,[1] one can scarcely demonstrate that the inner forme was first on the press throughout. Naturally, the probability will be high under the conditions outlined, but in its favour, actually, there is only a deduction supported by negative evidence from the headlines. In a different example, let us suppose that at the start, and again about midway, a book was demonstrably set by formes but no positive evidence was available about the setting of the intervening gatherings. The negative evidence that no change seemed to have occurred in the method of printing between the two points is not suitable for any other claim than probability that the book was set by formes throughout.

To repeat, probability in its different orders usually results when in some crucial part we must deduce the interpretation of the evidence from our knowledge of general printing practice, and when we cannot reason inductively from evidence throughout to recreate the terms of the printing method and thus reach the plane of the demonstrable. In these circumstances the bibliographical argument usually shifts its method at some point in the reasoning and—if it is honest—appeals openly to probability in the following manner:

[1] For this new and invaluable bibliographical technique see Kenneth Povey, 'The Optical Identification of First Formes', *Studies in Bibliography*, xiii (1960), 189–90.

some link is missing in the evidence directly relating the specific phenomenon to the general practice, but the concrete evidence in the text is not inconsistent with what we know would be produced by normal printing procedures and thus the missing link may be supplied by conjecture.

However disguised, this is ultimately an argument from analogy, and as such it has its dangers in bibliographical work. At its most dangerous, analogy is improperly employed to suggest a relationship between phenomena and general printing usage when there is no tangible evidence at all that such a relationship exists. At its best, analogy can be employed to supplement some partially established relationship between effect and presumed cause.[1]

The wrong use of analogy to conceal simple guess-work is found in Mr. Musgrove's recent attack on the problem why the proof-reader of sig. qq2^v of the First Folio *King Lear* changed the uncorrected Folio reading *sentence* to *sentences* in the Folio line 'To come betwixt our sentence, and our power' (1. i. 170). In brief, he conjectures that Q *betweene* was altered by the annotator of the printer's copy to *betwixt* (reproduced in F), and that Q *sentence* was also altered to *sentences* but that the Folio compositor overlooked the small addition of final -*s*. The Folio proof-reader, running his eye down the page, paused at any line where there was a correction in the Q copy and so picked up the manuscript change to the plural that the compositor had missed.[2]

Actually, we have no evidence that the primary assumption for the analogy is correct, which requires the Folio

---

[1] A typical case of dangerous analogy (when no partial relationship has been established) is Dover Wilson's explanation of the appearance in *Hamlet* Q2 (1. i. 55) of the misprint 'but' instead of the correct reading 'lust': the compositor chanced to omit the *s* and so produced the lost original reading *lut* which the proof-reader rationalized incorrectly as *but*. Since the case is hypothetical from start to finish, and evidence is wanting that the proof-reader concerned himself with this word, no relation of the misprint to the proof-reading process can be inferred. The analogy is meaningless, and the argument is not even one to rank as a speculative possibility.

[2] *Review of English Studies*, N.S., viii (1957), 170–1.

proof-reader to have read proof back against copy. After surveying all the variants that he has recovered, Dr. Hinman has found only a handful of formes in the entire Folio that give any reason to believe they were read against copy or referred to copy in any way, and sig. qq2^v is not among them. At the one end, therefore, the necessary fact about printing procedure that analogy should attach itself to is very likely wrong, and one's confidence in the suggested procedure is not increased by the dependent conjecture about the very odd method of reading proofs by checking only lines in which the printer's copy contained scribal alterations, an operation for which there is no evidence (internal or external).

As a consequence, no relationship can be established between the phenomenon to be explained (the alteration of a satisfactory singular to an unsatisfactory plural) and the precise method of proof-reading. The argument makes an initial dangerous assumption that *sentences* must be right because the proof-reader altered the original *sentence*; the critic then constructs out of thin air the complicated mechanical process which, if followed, could have brought about such a result. Thus in all circularity an assumption that *sentences* is right has been rationalized by a hypothetical reconstruction, and this reconstruction is then offered in the name of bibliography as the reason why future editors must restore the purity of Shakespeare's plural reading, no matter how little they like it.

Such a reconstruction in terms of the printing process may be hypothetically possible, but editors should beware of believing that it is therefore probable. In actual fact, this 'explanation' of how *sentences* could have been the copy-reading is so extravagantly improbable (to use Dr. Hinman's words) as to have no value in support of the alteration in the corrected state. Its attempted analogy that proof was read against copy is suspect, and it is devoid of any specific evidence relating the phenomenon to the specific method of reading against copy that was suggested.

VII. *The Probable: Some Uses of Analogy*

Any very close application of analogy without an immediate connexion with the book, or at least the shop (usually with the specific compositor), in question, has its very real dangers. Frequently, though not invariably, a proof-reader will call for many more alterations in the first reading than he will if he happens to return to the proofed page for a check and sees a few errors that he missed. But arguments for first or for second reading based on the number of variants may be quite misleading without some control to indicate what is normal for the book as a whole. Collation of 17 copies of Dekker's *2 Honest Whore* (1630) reveals 4 variant formes: 3 have 2 alterations each and 1 forme has a single variant. This low number does not necessarily mean that we have observed throughout only a second round of correction: it may well be that the proof-reader in his first survey found only these few errors that he thought worth correcting.

The habits of two proof-readers could differ very widely indeed. When in a book from another shop, *Match Me in London* (1631), we find 16 corrections in the first stage of the proof-alteration of inner C, 21 corrections in outer D, 10 in inner D, 21 in the first stage of inner F, and so on, grounds may exist for controlled analogy to suggest the *possibility* that the single variants in outer B and in outer E, and the 2 in outer G and outer I, represent second-round correction of an earlier corrected state that has not been recovered.

The conditions for controlled judgement here are manifestly of a different order from those in *2 Honest Whore*. But the evidence of *Match Me* is valid only within its own pages (or possibly for its proof-reader if he could be spotted elsewhere). It has little or no validity in any attempt to evaluate the proof-reading of *2 Honest Whore*.

At its best, analogy operates under conditions when (*a*) we can be very sure indeed of the absolute nature of the general printing practice appealed to and the likelihood of its application to the evidence at hand (as Mr. Musgrove was not sure); or (*b*) when the analogy is hitched at its farther end not to general practice but to the observed operation of an identified shop and (if he is involved) with the observed operation of one or more identified workmen within that shop, as witness the proof-reader of *Match Me*.

(*a*) We may certainly have some confidence in our knowledge of certain features of the printing process in Shakespeare's day. At a very elementary plane purely for an example, we may be sure that a four-leaf gathering in a squarish book of quarto size was printed from eight regularly imposed type-pages in two formes on a full sheet of paper if the first and fourth and also the second and third leaves are conjugate, if a watermark appears in one half of the sheet and therefore in the inner margin of either one of the two folds that comprise the gathering, if the chain-lines are horizontal, and if the regular gatherings preceding and succeeding are similarly constructed.

But it is proper to point out, as was noticed in the section about normality and its postulate, that some of the printing procedures we have had strongest belief in have proved far from invariable. For instance, the new knowledge that many books were set by formes rather than seriatim has forced a complete review of many important assumptions. Hence one should be conservative in asserting the absoluteness of our knowledge about any detail of the printing process until the whole matter has been very thoroughly explored.

(*b*) The critic is on stronger ground when he can appeal to analogy within parts of the same book, or to the observed practices of the same compositor, or at the very least to the observed operations of the same printing-house. It is dangerous in the extreme to apply loose generalizations about the usual practices of undiscriminated workmen to explain by attempted analogy some particular phenomenon. Palaeographical accounts of textual error are often guilty of this sort of reasoning. The theoretical possibility that certain

letter formations, or certain combinations of letter formations, will in such hands as Secretary or Italian be misread as certain other letters is the necessary palaeographical
assumption, sometimes demonstrated to be true. But possibility is not probability—one must continue to repeat—and
analogies between textual errors and hypothesized letter
formations are frequently inexact. The lack of any scientific
control in the method is well illustrated by Mr. Sisson's
rationalization of *thereby* in Q2 *Hamlet* as a possible compositorial misreading of manuscript *shortly*, whereas we
know for a fact that *thereby* was the proof-reader's independent alteration of a word that the compositor had set as
thirtie from whatever was the manuscript form. In reprints
many errors are found that are identical with those supposed
to have derived from misread handwriting. And Sir Walter
Greg's observation that the assumption of handwriting
error is more useful after the correction than before, doubtless reflected some dissatisfaction with any scientific pretensions in a method that must always depend upon analogy
and accompanying hypothesis for the interpretation of
evidence.

The 'bibliographical' recovery of a manuscript spelling,
like Dr. Walker's identification of *chaples* in the manuscript
of *Romeo and Juliet* Q2, should not be confused with the
quite dissimilar method of palaeographical criticism, the
explanation of a misreading by the postulate that a particular
form of a spelling existed in the printer's copy.

An example occurs in John Donne's *Divine Poems* edited
in 1952 by Helen Gardner. In line 61 of 'A Litanie' Donne
prays that 'thy Patriarckes Desire' may 'Be satisfied and
fructifie in mee'. At least this is the reading of the 1633
edition, supported by two good manuscripts from Group I,
as against *sanctified* in all other manuscripts. Miss Gardner
comments (page 85) that the other manuscripts' *sanctified*
'is explicable as a misreading if the spelling were "sattisfied".
The first "t" might be read as a "c", and its cross-bar taken

as a suspension over the "a". The "sf" would then be read as "ff".'

Some useful points can be made from this palaeographical suggestion in order to emphasize the peculiar nature of bibliography. In a discussion of misreading in textual transmission in manuscript, ordinarily (as here) the manuscript in which the error first occurred is lost or unidentified. Thus the characteristics of the scribe cannot be recovered in any detail, and the critic has no concrete evidence from which to estimate other possibilities. In textual transmission through printed books, where we are generally safe in the belief that no examples have been lost, we can (in contrast) identify the document in which the misreading occurred and therefore we can analyse the characteristics of the human agent through whose head and hands the text passed.

It was the ability to do just this to the compositor in question of Q2 *Romeo and Juliet* that alone made Dr. Walker's case for *chaples* so binding, because this man's ascertained spelling habits prevented the critic from accepting as a possibility a very easy alternative explanation: the simple transposition of two letters. When two equally good possibilities clash, any decision can be only speculative. Dr. Walker's ability to eliminate the alternative possibility had the result of promoting the survivor to the rank of 'highly probable'.

In contrast, Miss Gardner offered only one narrow possibility, a misreading, and did not consider the equally acceptable alternative of sophistication (whether conscious or inadvertent through memorial error). Since *sanctified* makes tempting sense, perhaps one a little more obvious than *satisfied*, scribal error for reasons other than palaeographical is at the very least a paired argument. As a consequence, it is futile to attempt to reconstruct the manuscript spelling as a form of evidence, for quite possibly the spelling was not in any way the source of the variant.

Indeed, even if we were to rig the odds here for the sake

of illustration and to accept (what is unacceptable) the greater possibility that simple misreading created the error, we should be still as uncertain about the spelling of the manuscript. The reason is not far to seek. Palaeographical 'explanations' have a marked tendency to take it for granted that every letter must be confused with another, as if the scribe were puzzling out the word in detail, letter by letter, and consistently getting it wrong. On the contrary, any bibliographer familiar with the habits of compositors knows that a copyist in any medium has a number of influences working on him, ranging from the visual or aural message that the formation of the letters gives him to the force of the context; and constantly exerting a pressure is the tendency to see what he anticipates he will see. Or, to be more precise, to see what the first general impression of the letter shapes transmits to him. Any copyist makes a series of running jumps at words, in this manner. Thus misreading is seldom simple, and error results usually from the influence of only a few letters that transmit an erroneous picture of the whole word to the brain.

Accustomed as he is to this process in reprints, under conditions in which the letter-by-letter misreading posited by palaeographers is impossible, no bibliographer would dare to argue for *sattisfied* as the manuscript spelling that created the variant. First, intentional variation by the copyist to improve the meaning, in his own opinion, is as acceptable a hypothesis if not a superior one. Second, even if misreading were to be settled on, *sanctified* is almost as possible a mistake for *satisfied* as for *sattisfied*. Too many intangibles enter such a case for any certainty to hold. For this reason palaeographical arguments are usually only rationalizations of good editorial guesses and cannot be compared in their validity to bibliographical reasoning from concrete evidence by which textual critics may sometimes recover certain features of the spelling of lost manuscript copy through analysis of the spelling characteristics of an identified compositor.

Bibliographers are by no means innocent of playing fast

and loose with analogy, however, and nowhere less than in the discussion of the habits of compositors. That 'compositors' would follow the spellings of their copy more faithfully when at leisure than in haste or when in haste than at leisure; that 'compositors' so carefully reproduced the copy markings for metrical elision that the characteristics of the manuscript can be recovered with accuracy from the print; that 'compositors' seldom reproduced the accidental features of their copy, or that 'compositors' were in general reasonably faithful to the accidentals—these are all generalized opinions that are not only untested (usually) by evidence that can be taken seriously but are also (usually) untestable in some major part when applied in general terms to a concrete problem.

Some compositorial habits may be so uniform as to be susceptible of generalization. It is very likely true that a prose line was usually justified by the alteration of spelling, perhaps in some conjunction with the adjustment of the thickness of spaces between words, whereas a verse line not filling the measure was justified ordinarily among its quads and spaces in the white at the right margin. This is a reasonable deduction, and there is some scattered evidence to support it. Nevertheless, before it can be generally accepted it must be inductively proved from concrete evidence in a series of printing-houses. That is, the work of a number of identified compositors must be studied to discover whether their characteristic spellings are more uniform in verse than in prose, and whether (to refine the evidence) their spelling characteristics in full lines of verse are less uniform than in short lines.

What information we have suggests that this generalization will hold among several identified compositors, that their spelling habits are indeed less pure in prose than in verse, and that full lines of verse may indeed affect the characteristics of their spelling. Dr. Hinman, for example, has shown that the conventional *do–go–here* tests for

Compositors A and B in the Folio are remarkably trustworthy when account is taken of the length of the line in which the words appear, and that anomalies are more likely to be found in lines taking up the full measure than in short lines. This is excellent evidence, for Compositors A and B are becoming old friends to us and they serve as very good guinea-pigs for the study of variation. Moreover, the results here, so far as they have been carried, appear to be strengthened by such spelling tests as Dr. J. R. Brown has applied to James Roberts' Compositors X and Y, whose prominent characteristics have a tendency to become more diffuse in prose than in verse.[1]

On the other hand, to date no identified compositor has been exhaustively studied (as by the application of an electronic computer to the problem) to permit us to generalize even about one man's characteristics when setting from printed or from manuscript copy, let alone whether he was in haste or working at a normal pace. Moreover, it is surely idle to generalize about compositorial treatment of metrical elision without applying what control texts there are to a study of the particular compositors who set them before assuming, by analogy, that with what one workman does another will surely coincide. Indeed, the most elementary test for compositorial treatment of such matters as metrical elision has not been brought to bear. This is the assessment of a specific compositor's characteristics when setting a reprint. One or two experiments of this kind, including some experience with Folio Compositor E, have convinced me that it is possible for a workman to diverge often enough from his copy in respect to elision as to make assumptions dangerous that the characteristics of the copy in this respect can be recovered from a print with any trustworthy accuracy.[2]

---

[1] 'The Compositors of *Hamlet* Q2 and *The Merchant of Venice*', *Studies in Bibliography*, vii (1955), 32 ff.

[2] This experience with control reprint texts has made me cautious of accepting the conclusions of H. T. Price, 'Author, Compositor, and Metre: Copy-Spellings in "Titus Andronicus" and other Elizabethan Printings', *Papers of the Bibliographical Society of America*, 53 (1959), 160–87.

Finally, the justifying of lines by the use of spaces of different widths, as against the alteration of spellings, has not been studied. We do not know from sufficient evidence whether words are more irregularly spaced in verse than in prose, or in full lines of verse as against short lines, in the work of any one workman. Nor do we know very much about the relation of such evidence to the act of setting a line in comparison to the tinkering with methods for justifying after completion of the line.

Until a sufficient number of diverse workmen are studied in considerable technical detail, we shall all be well advised to deduce as cautiously as we can from our own imperfect notions about such matters as the effect of various conditions on compositorial characteristics (especially in relation to the setting from manuscript or from print), for at present we are employing analogy in a manner that is not in the best traditions of scholarship.

NOTES

Note A, p. 71. For example, J. Dover Wilson (*MSH*, i. 144) asks us to believe that when we find the folio line in *Hamlet*, i. iii. 3, in the form 'And Conuoy is assistant; doe not sleepe', and a comma misplaced in the variant Q2 line, 'And conuay, in assistant doe not sleepe', we may guess that the press-corrector has shuffled the position of the punctuation in an attempt to make sense of a doubly misprinted Q2 line. The postulate of normality requires us, instead, to assume that errors in a text proceed from the compositor, unless direct evidence from observed press-variants leads us to the person of the cor-rector. In this instance the Folio compositor could have misinterpreted the line (especially if Q2 were the copy) just as readily as a corrector; or perhaps the annotator of Q2 could have been responsible. Since no supporting evidence suggests the corrector, it is not suitable to assign an irregularity like this to his unpredictable human failure in a routine process.

Note B, p. 80. This problem is essentially different from that of the half-sheet in *Match Me in London*. In that quarto there was every reason to assume continuous printing of the preliminaries following on the body of the text. Hence when the running-title pattern indicated that something else had been printed with the final half-sheet of the text, it would have been fantasy indeed to speculate that this something might have been (instead) a part of some other book, the preliminaries being machined later as a separate half-sheet. The inductive reasoning should be clear. The pattern of running-titles indicates that the final half-sheet of the text was not machined by single half-sheet imposition. We do not need to appeal to general printing practice, however, to deduce that the something else printed with it was the pre-liminaries. The pattern of the watermarks, in this case aided by the shared stages of alteration in the appropriate formes of both half-sheets, provides the evidence by which we arrive at the conclusion that the preliminaries were printed with the final half-sheet. In *Troilus and Cressida* the fact that a cancel in the preliminaries is in question leaves the time element in some doubt (as it is not in *Match Me*), and one could not almost automatically deduce that the 'something else' printed with the final half-sheet must have been the two-leaf cancel. Hence specific evidence to associate the two *Troilus* half-sheets is the more necessary if inductive reasoning is to obtain; and fortunately the evidence of the division of watermarks is available for this purpose.

Note C, p. 80. If, as is not true, all examples of the cancel fold had used a different watermark from that found invariably in the body of the book, and especially in half-sheet M in all preserved exemplars, then—of course—we should be close to demonstration (if not already there) that half-sheets ¶ and M were *not* printed together as a full sheet and then cut apart; but we could only adduce the possibility that a lapse of time had occurred between the machining of M and then of ¶. We could not rest the case on the assumption that the change in watermark must have resulted from the exhaustion of the regular paper over the passage of time. For all we know, the machining of M could have used up practically all the paper that had been ordered, and ¶ could have followed on the press immediately but with a change in the paper stock. The evidence concerning the time-connexion would have been insufficient to bear the weight of the interpretation.

Note D, p. 82. That the order is correct and that an originally set damaged letter was not replaced with an undamaged type as part of the process of proof-correction can be shown by the Hinman Collating Machine, which reveals no movement of types in this area such as would have occurred if one sort had been substituted for another. This is concrete evidence, even of a negative kind, but it may be supported by other kinds of evidence even though these do not appear in the page in question and therefore involve an appeal to printing practice. However, here the appeal is somewhat more precise than usual in that the analogy is indicated not with general printing procedures but instead with the specific methods observed elsewhere in the same book. Dr. Hinman observes, for example, that in the known press-variant formes of the Folio when changes were being made in other matters, the correctors did not mark any damaged type for replacement even though they concerned themselves with other typographical trivia. Second, the press-variants in a Folio forme are seldom single, as is the variant in this page. Moreover, during the whole course of printing the Folio the correctors or the pressmen never anywhere else interrupted the printing merely to replace a damaged type. The force of the evidence for a lack of displacement surrounding the type is partly reduced by the negative quality of the evidence. If displacement *had* been observed, we should have had positive specific evidence of the highest order in favour of the priority of the damaged type; but the absence of normally expected phenomena is not so cogent an argument in favour of the priority of the undamaged piece. None the less, although each one of these three varieties of evidence is singly only a movement in the direction of possibility, Dr. Hinman feels that their combination is weighty enough to support the confident statement that the 'd' on sig. m6 represents two states of the identical piece of type, before and after injury. It then follows that the forme m1^v.6 must have preceded through the press any other forme of the Folio containing the damaged 'd'. Thus sig. m6 must have been set and printed earlier than sig. d3^v, despite the fact that gathering m is further along in the Folio than gathering d. Because of the importance of the conclusion, it is fortunate, however, that this particular problem need not depend for solution only on this correlation of evidence: Dr. Hinman's analysis of the printer's cases and their exact contents of damaged types demonstrates by any number of irreversible facts that the order of the formes is that stated above, with m preceding d.

IV

THE INTERPRETATION OF EVIDENCE:
THE PROBABLE

Except when analogy within the same book[1] is appealed to under logically controlled conditions, an attempt to substitute the postulate of normality for a demonstrated relationship between evidence and operation is almost always unsatisfactory. Our knowledge of printing is not usually so complete that we can assure ourselves:

(1) That the printing process was uniform in the particular respect under analysis so that given a certain assumed operation an invariable order of result would be produced.

(2) That whereas the operation was uniform (we may suppose), no alternative accepted method existed that could produce the same physical phenomena in the book under examination.

(3) That the evidence being surveyed is not so narrow or unique as to introduce the possibility of aberration—of human variation from the norm, or of human failure.

(4) That the number of extant copies of the book is not too small for us to observe the evidence in sufficient depth, that is, to gain the necessary perspective for a just estimate of the evidence that has been discovered, or else to enable us to develop supplementary evidence of the kind that can be found in the examination of multiple copies.

(5) That even when we may be fairly certain about the details of the printing operation, it may yet be possible to

[1] Or in some instances within the product of the same identified workman operating under similar conditions in other books. Jaggard's Compositor B has substantially the same characteristics in the First Folio as in the earlier Pavier Quartos. For a sampling of the evidence, see D. F. McKenzie, 'Compositor B's Role in *The Merchant of Venice* Q2 (1619)', *Studies in Bibliography*, xii (1958), 75–89.

make more than one reasonable interpretation of the evidence—not necessarily in respect to the physical printing process itself but instead to the causes for the operation or the agents who ordered or performed it.

Whenever a bibliographical problem comes under one or other of these headings, the uncertainty is likely to be too great for *probability* to be admitted unless there is some special corroboration. The category of *possibility* is ordinarily the proper one.

1. *Uniformity of the Printing Process*

(1) To secure certainty, and even probability, we should be satisfied that the printing operation was uniform in respect to the detail under analysis. For example, if the compositor(s) set the type-pages of a book in seriatim order, and if the same two skeletons were used to impose the inner and outer formes of every sheet, we could be relatively certain that an invariant forme backing a variant forme exhibits a corrected state of the type (granting that proof were read) and that the same agent would have ordered the alterations in both formes. We may believe that we know this because under these conditions the proof-reading of the two formes would, in effect, have been continuous.

On the other hand, if the same conditions held (including the use of one press) except that the sheets had been set by formes from cast-off copy (various of the pages being composed out of seriatim order), the interpretation of the evidence would be completely reversed: a matter of hours, not of minutes, would have separated the respective times of proof-reading the two formes, and hence from this mechanical evidence no inferences could be made whether the corrector of each forme were the same or a different reader. Moreover, in a book set by formes the second forme to be placed on the press will not normally be invariant, and any press-alterations it exhibits are more likely to represent the first rather than a second round of correction. As a consequence, unless for each sheet of a book we can secure evidence whether the pages were set in order or else by formes, we cannot relate the proof-reading of the two formes to each other with any probability.

Another example may be cited. In a two-skeleton quarto set seriatim by a single compositor, the delivery to the press and machining of the outer forme of a sheet before the inner forme ought to indicate that the compositor was comfortably ahead of the press since he had been able to finish 4^v before any forme of the sheet was required by the pressman. On the other hand, in a similar quarto consistently set by formes, the order of the formes sent to the press might have no significance as evidence about the compositor–press relationship: under these conditions composition of both formes could never be completed, ordinarily, before the press would require the initial forme of the sheet. Hence conclusions about compositorial speed based on the evidence of the order of the formes through the press are worthless unless one knows how the quarto was typeset.[1]

11. *Alternative Methods of Printing*

(2) Certainty and even probability are materially reduced when methodical variation within an ascertainably uniform operation would produce the same physical evidence in a book so that without supplementary information one has only a fifty per cent. chance of correctly interpreting the known facts.

---

[1] Dr. R. K. Turner, Jr., has shown that such odd patterns in books set by formes as the regular alternation in successive sheets of inner and outer formes first sent to press has little or nothing to do with the time factor and seems to have been dictated by theoretical convenience in dealing with copy. But the full reasons for this pattern are still somewhat obscure owing to our sketchy information. See Turner, 'The Printing of Beaumont and Fletcher's *The Maid's Tragedy* Q1 (1619)', *Studies in Bibliography*, xiii (1960), 206–7, 215. Perhaps some relation exists between this practice and that in the Shakespeare First Folio whereby a compositor working on the second half of one gathering would continue and set the first half of the next gathering, his partner (who had set the first half) skipping to set the second half of the next.

Dekker's *Old Fortunatus* (1600) is a quarto printed throughout with only one skeleton, and therefore both formes of any sheet might show press-corrections. Yet collation of the eleven extant copies reveals only two very minor alterations, each in a different sheet. It is faintly possible that the compositor was so careful in his typesetting that these were the only errors that the proof-reader noticed and chose to correct. On the other hand, if the printer had been very much concerned to print only from corrected type,[1] he could have varied the proofing operation systematically so that the press was idle while proof was being read. Thus no uncorrected states of any forme would normally be produced, and the two known variants would represent a second round of alteration (less likely, in reverse, the errors made by carelessly repaired pulled types). If we had nothing more than the simple evidence of these two variants that could have resulted from either way of handling the proof-reading process, we should find ourselves hard put to know whether the type throughout had or had not been proof-read in the invariant sheets.

As another example, when one has established the seriatim typesetting of a book printed with two skeletons, and when variants appear in both formes of a sheet, the usual inference one draws is that the variants in the forme first on the press will represent the initial press-correction, and the variants in the opposite forme will represent a second round of proof-reading, since normally this latter forme would be invariant.

In the proofing operation with two skeletons (and

---

[1] A desire to vary an operation in order to secure correctness in a maximum number of sheets is not unknown in seventeenth-century printing. For example, the proof-reading of Shakespeare's First Folio was far from careful, as Dr. Hinman has shown. Yet it is clear that for some sheets the proof-reader sent corrected proof back when only one page of the folio forme had been read. The press was stopped, the compositor altered the type in this page, and printing was resumed until the proof-reader had finished the second page, whereupon the routine was repeated. See C. J. K. Hinman, 'The Proof-Reading of the First Folio Text of *Romeo and Juliet*', *Studies in Bibliography*, vi (1954), 63 and references.

seriatim-set pages) the forme first sent to the press prints a proof and then the press proceeds to manufacture uncorrected states of the white-paper forme until such time as the proof is read and returned. The press is then stopped and the white-paper forme removed for correction. In the interval the perfecting forme will ordinarily have been completed, and this is placed on the press and proofs are pulled while the white-paper forme is being altered. The white-paper forme is then returned to the press in its corrected state to complete its part of the machining of the edition-sheet. During this time the perfecting forme has been corrected from its returned proof, and thus when it is placed on the press and perfects the edition-sheet in one operation, all the sheets that this forme impresses will be invariant unless proof is read a second time (or some error detected) and the press is stopped during the perfecting for another correction of the type. As a consequence, the appearance of press-variants in the perfecting forme would ordinarily signify re-read proof and further alteration.

However, if composition of the perfecting forme were delayed beyond the point when corrected proof was returned for the white-paper forme on the press, the printer might perhaps decide to continue printing from the uncorrected white-paper forme on the press until the opposite forme was ready for proofing. In this circumstance identical results would obtain with what we may take to be the customary method, except that the proportion of uncorrected to corrected states would be higher than usual.[1]

---

[1] What is 'usual' may be difficult to decide, even for the same book, owing to the small number of copies ordinarily obtainable and collated, and the consequent statistical distortion of the evidence. One should also remark that a high proportion of uncorrected states is by no means sound evidence for a hypothesis that the opposite forme was late. Just as possibly, the assigned reader was not in the shop when printing started on the white-paper forme and thus the reading of the proof was delayed. The physical evidence would be the same, and hence one interpretation is no more possible than the other. Of course, a bibliographer might believe, according to his experience, that the absent-proof-reader hypothesis was generally the more plausible; but he could not prove it.

On the contrary, if the printer were concerned to reduce the uncorrected pulls of his white-paper forme to a minimum despite a delay in completing the opposite forme, he might (we may suppose) proceed with the correction of this forme as early as possible and resume printing. The pulling of proofs and the correction of the perfecting forme could then be reserved until such time as (*a*) it was placed on the press for make-ready to perfect the edition-sheet, or (*b*) it was introduced for a few pulls during the printing of the white-paper forme with or without an occasion offered by a second round of alteration to the white-paper forme.[1] If the type were not corrected (as in (*a*) above) until the perfecting forme was actually on the press and ready to machine the edition-sheet, the basic proofing method would revert to that of one-skeleton imposition, with its attendant delays, and the results would agree in that both formes of a sheet would exhibit uncorrected states as well as corrected. Yet there are no known bibliographical tests to prevent the critic from misinterpreting the evidence under these variant conditions that might develop occasionally within the uniform two-skeleton printing process. Confusion could easily arise, therefore, in evaluating the perfecting forme's uncorrected state as one that had already been proof-read, and its first-round alterations as, instead, a second round of revision.[2] Some quite wrong textual assumptions might readily follow from such an error.

1 Moxon describes a method of pulling proofs that interrupted the printing whenever a forme to be proofed was prepared. The delay would not be equally serious, but on the evidence this does not seem to have been the usual Elizabethan practice.

2 Ordinarily a second round of revision will produce fewer variants than the first. Typical in Dekker's *Match Me in London* (1631) is inner C with 16 variants in the initial correction as against 7 in the second; or inner F with 21 in the first round as against 11 in the second. Or Dekker's *Magnificent Entertainment* (1604), which has 7 in outer H followed by 3 in the second round and 2 in the third. But the relationship is not invariable, and thus statistical evidence of this sort can seldom be ranked as affording high probability. For instance, in Dekker's *Whore of Babylon* (1607) the proportion in inner K is 2 and 2; in inner H of *The Magnificent Entertainment* (1604) the figures are only 4 and 3; in *The Wonder of a Kingdom* (1636) inner A has 26 in the first round and 28 in the second, though only 2 in the third.

In this same category one may mention still another phenomenon associated with the proof-reading. We know that the heap of printed white-paper sheets was turned over before perfecting so that the pressman was provided with a pile in which the sheets were most conveniently in position for placing on the pins in printing the opposite forme. If the whole pile of white-paper sheets had been turned over before any perfecting began,[1] the earliest sheets of the printed white-paper forme would invariably be on top of the reversed pile and would therefore be backed by the earliest impressions of the perfecting forme.

Let us assume, for convenience, that the white-paper forme is the inner, and the perfecting forme is the outer. If machining of the outer forme were interrupted for proof-correction before the number of sheets had been exhausted that contained the white-paper forme in the uncorrected state, some sheets would show the uncorrected states of both formes, others would show the corrected outer backed by the uncorrected inner, and still others the corrected inner perfected by the corrected outer. Correspondingly, if machining of the outer forme were stopped, instead, for proof-correction after the uncorrected states of the inner forme had all been perfected, some sheets would contain the uncorrected states of both formes, some the corrected inner backed by the uncorrected outer, and others the corrected states of both.

If we could be sure that the heap was always completely turned before perfecting began, strict bibliographical interpretation could often decide all questions of critical doubt as to which state would be the corrected and which not. Whenever there is an overlap and one state of a forme is backed by two states of the opposite forme, it is necessary only to determine the order of the states of one of these formes to assure ourselves of the order of the others. To illustrate (Fig. 1):

---

[1] It would be indifferent whether the whole heap were turned over at once in a very small impression, or whether in a larger the heap were turned before perfecting by the series of operations that Moxon calls 'grasps'.

if the manifestly uncorrected state of the inner forme were
backed by two undetermined states of the outer forme, the
true corrected state of the outer must be that one that also
backs the corrected state of the inner forme since it alone
could have continued down the heap to perfect the remaining
sheets. (Figs. 1, &c., show the heap of sheets as if viewed
from the side on the level. Diagram (*a*) indicates the finished

FIGURE I

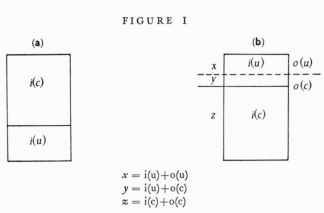

$$x = i(u)+o(u)$$
$$y = i(u)+o(c)$$
$$z = i(c)+o(c)$$

heap of white-paper sheets before it is turned for perfecting;
diagram (*b*) indicates this same heap completely turned at
the moment the run would be prepared to begin perfecting.
A dotted line indicates the course taken by the perfecting
outer forme.)

Correspondingly (Fig. 2), if the indubitable uncorrected
state of the inner forme were backed by only one state of the
outer, but the corrected state of the inner were opposed by
two states of the outer, that forme of the outer that bridges
both corrected and uncorrected inner must be the earlier and
thus the uncorrected state.

These conclusions are reversible so that they cover the determination of the order of correction in the white-paper forme
when the order of the perfecting forme is known. Moreover,
given the right conditions they could be utilized to show the
order of two or more rounds of correction in one forme.

On this physical basis the reasoning is so inexorable that one could easily be tempted to believe any conclusions drawn from such evidence to be firm and demonstrated. But, unfortunately, we have recently learned that certain details concerning the turning over of the heap of paper for perfecting need not have been invariable. Certainty about conclusions based on invariable operation, hence, has been considerably

FIGURE 2

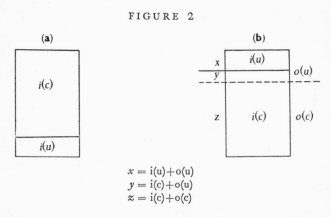

$$x = i(u)+o(u)$$
$$y = i(c)+o(u)$$
$$z = i(c)+o(c)$$

modified. It is true that the available evidence suggests that in many shops (or perhaps by many workmen) the heap was in fact turned completely before perfecting began. Thus in six Dekker plays from the canon, thirteen sheets that are known to be variant in both formes agree without difficulty with this reasoning, except for one of these plays, *Match Me in London* (1631), in which one sheet refuses to fit into the pattern. In sheet F the Newberry Library copy shows the inner forme in the first-stage-of-correction state, and the Hyde copy shows the uncorrected. But the outer forme of the Newberry is in the uncorrected and of the Hyde in the corrected state, an impossible situation if the pile had been completely turned before perfecting began. Reference above to Fig. 1 will show that the Hyde copy would be *y*, but the Newberry copy could not exist. In Fig. 2 if the Newberry copy were *y*, the Hyde could not exist.

This one anomaly that I have observed might be a sport
(like an extra proof pull left over); but Dr. Hinman informs
me that in the Shakespeare First Folio the association of the
corrected and uncorrected states of sheets with both formes
variant is sometimes quite random and therefore equally
anomalous. Our information is too limited to generalize.
None the less, it is clear that whatever may have been the
usual practice, in some shops at least the heap might not
always be completely turned before perfecting began and
hence we cannot postulate an invariably uniform operation.

Only a few irregular sheets would be produced if the heap
were turned by a continuous series of 'grasps' while perfecting
was in process. Many more would be machined if there were
intervals between the 'grasps', or the turning of various
tokens of white-paper sheets—or even if only one such
interval occurred. For example, if perfecting began towards
the end of a working day and only one or two grasps were
made to see the press through the day's stint, the latest
printed sheets would be the first perfected. Or for some
reason or other the whole heap might not be turned at once
by a series of grasps, but instead a token or two might be left
unturned until later. Then this first-printed group of sheets
at the bottom of the original white-paper pile might be
turned and added to the heap while perfecting was in progress.
If this happened these particular sheets would be perfected
out of phase, and an uncorrected state of the white-paper
forme could easily be perfected by a corrected state of the
outer even though the outer had not been corrected until
after the uncorrected states of the white-paper forme in the
heap as first constituted for perfecting had been exhausted.
So many possibilities appear that purely bibliographical
evidence for the order of alteration could be quite misleading
if based on too few copies. Certainly if in sheet F of *Match
Me* we had preserved only two copies showing any press-
variants—the Newberry copy with the uncorrected state of
the inner forme and the Hyde with the uncorrected state of

the outer forme—the case for priority would be indeterminable on bibliographical grounds. Even more dangerous, if the examples with both formes uncorrected had not been known, we should have interpreted the printing in a very different way, and our conclusions would be different again if either the Newberry or else the Hyde copy had not been observed.[1]

Fortunately the incomplete evidence we have suggests that perfecting did not proceed through a heap that was occasionally turned in small groups of tokens as needed. If such bit-by-bit perfecting had been the method, the tokens would have been perfected roughly in their reverse order of printing, instead of in the same order as by standard operation. From such a procedure we should seldom if ever find an uncorrected state of the printing forme backed by an uncorrected state of the perfecting forme, since the earliest state of the printing forme would be among the last to be perfected. However, in some of the observed anomalous sheets we do indeed find uncorrected backed by uncorrected formes; and this evidence demonstrates that for these sheets enough of the heap had been turned before perfecting began (or else before the perfecting was stopped for press-alteration) to expose some of the uncorrected states of the white-paper forme in the lower part of the printed heap. This conclusion must be valid even though some part of the very bottommost uncorrected white-paper sheets in the original heap was not turned for perfecting until a substantial interval of time had passed, sufficient to allow for proof-reading and press-correction of the perfecting forme.[2]

---

[1] The facts about the press-variants in this sheet and their appearance in the twenty-five observed copies will be found in *The Dramatic Works of Thomas Dekker*, iii (1951), 351–3.

[2] One cannot make absolute statements about the precise details. For example, if perfecting began while sections of the heap were being turned in a continuous process, a very few corrected sheets from what had been the top of the white-paper heap would be perfected with the uncorrected state before the 'grasps' of the lower-lying uncorrected white-paper sheets were placed on the top of the fully turned

So far as can be reconstructed at the moment—and I believe that Dr. Hinman agrees in this interpretation of the Folio evidence—the heap seems to have been turned initially very much as a unit (although in several 'grasps'), but occasionally some of the bottom sheets were not added to the turned heap until an appreciably later time. It is odd, however, that once having engaged himself to turn the heap the workman did not continue with the relatively few minutes that would be required to finish the job.

One point is clear, I think. Given the danger of offsetting, as remarked by Moxon, it would usually be impracticable to turn only a few tokens of the heap before starting to perfect, for then the most recently printed sheets with the ink still at its freshest would be offered to the press. Ideally, the whole heap would be turned so that the earliest printed sheets at the very bottom would then be at the top, and offsetting would be at its least troublesome. However, we know from the work-and-turn method of printing by half-sheet imposition that the difficulties of offset could be surmounted if only half the normal printing (which is to say drying) time were allowed. Thus if the turning of the pile of paper were interrupted on some occasions, it would seem that perfecting would be quite practicable so long as one-half or more of the heap had been prepared for machining on its opposite side. And this is, in fact, what the available statistics suggest: that in each case more than one-half of the heap had been turned before perfecting was begun.

We can only speculate why in various instances some part of the heap was left unturned until a later time. If we are to guess, I would suggest the following possibility. The preparation of the press for perfecting involved the removal of

heap. But there would have been very few, and perhaps (if a problem would arise from offsetting) the relatively few minutes saved would not be worth the trouble created. If such sheets were perfected, and by chance preserved, they might betray themselves by an anomalous combination of the states of their formes, but sometimes they might be indistinguishable from sheets regularly perfected somewhat later. The matter is certainly obscure.

the preceding forme and its washing, the locking-in of the perfecting forme accompanied by the make-ready and various trials, and the substitution of a cloth covering for the parchment of the tympan. If the pressman's assistant were unable to complete his duties here, and at the same time by a series of 'grasps' to turn all of the pile of paper before the press was ready to begin perfecting, rather than hold up work the pressman might decide to start perfecting so long as a sufficient number of tokens had been turned to present no serious offsetting problem in the sheets immediately available for machining. In such an event the assistant would turn the remaining sheets and add them to the top of the heap during any subsequent interruption, like washing down the tympan covering, stopping the press for correction of type, or at the end of a day's work. Such a normal irregularity might seem to offer a hypothetical explanation for the apparent anomaly of sheets that were occasionally perfected out of phase.

This technical bibliographical problem, minor as it may be, is not an entirely sterile one for textual criticism. By such an analysis of problems in the light of our information—thus extended—about the variation possible within the printing process, an editor can explain the otherwise inexplicable combinations of states in variant formes like those in sheet F of *Match Me in London* and thus avoid idle speculation about their causes. He will certainly learn to be wary of over-confident assertions about the relation between two variant formes in the same sheet without evidence from more copies than have usually been thought necessary.[1] If he were uncertain about the order of the different states within any one forme, like F in *Match Me*, the bibliographical reconstruction shown in Fig. 3 would set him straight, where literary evidence might be ambiguous. And when the evidence of the Povey–Martin lamp, or of the distribution and setting of identifiable types, assists in establishing the order of the formes on the press, the critic faced with textual variation

[1] See note A, pp. 130–1.

may reach to a precision of information available by no other means.

The determination of the order of the formes on the press is a very important matter for a book set page after page in seriatim sequence and imposed by two skeleton-formes. Under these conditions the decision whether the initial stage of observed press-alteration in either forme is the original or, in fact, a second round (the original being unknown), depends directly upon establishing which was the first forme sent to the press and which the perfecting forme. And when he is faced with a sophisticating proof-reader such as the one who worked over *Match Me*, an editor will certainly want to know whether he can trust the so-called 'uncorrected' state of the type in a forme to be the compositor's original typesetting that has not been tampered with by another agent, or whether he may be able to conjecture on a sound bibliographical basis that readings set from the manuscript by the compositor could have been altered by the proof-reader. This is another example of how bibliography can set up conditions under which criticism must operate, and I can testify from personal experience that it is one of some practical significance.

In a quarto set by formes, as in *Match Me*, the gain may be somewhat more theoretical, for the order of the formes can usually have nothing to do with the method of proof-reading, as it has with seriatim-set books. However, some useful inferences can be made, once the exact order is established for the sheets in the perfecting heap. For example, the proportion of four to one in the observed *yb* as against the *ya* state indicates the excellent possibility that the outer forme was press-corrected only once, despite the double correction of the inner; and hence that its 'uncorrected' readings are indeed in all details what the compositor set from manuscript, with no concealed intervention such as might have occurred in a lost initial stage of correction. If the pages had been seriatim-set, it would be almost a certainty (on the evidence of the Povey–Martin lamp that the inner forme was first through

FIGURE 3

The evidence from 25 observed copies is as follows:

inner (u) xa —— ya outer (u) 4 copies
inner (c^1) xb^1 —— yb outer (c) 5 copies
inner (c^2) xb^2 —— yb outer (c) 14 copies
inner (c^1) xb^1 —— ya outer (u) 1 copy (Newberry)
inner (u) xa —— yb outer (c) 1 copy (Hyde)

PRINTED ON ONE PRESS

INNER FORME FIRST

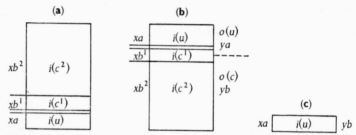

The Newberry sheet results when *ya* perfects a few copies of xb^1. The Hyde copy results when the unturned bottom *xa* sheets in a small separate pile are turned and placed on the heap at some unknown time after the correction of the outer forme. If the outer forme were corrected before the uncorrected *xa* sheets were exhausted, the Hyde sheet could result from the perfecting of the remaining *xa* sheets with the corrected outer forme (*yb*). But then no explanation for the Newberry copy is possible, for any separate small pile of inner-forme sheets would need to be in state xb^1. The Povey–Martin lamp indicates that the inner forme was indeed first on the press.

OUTER FORME FIRST (hypothetical)

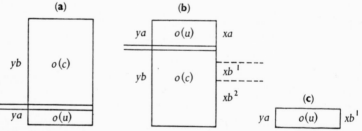

The Hyde sheet results when *xa* perfects a few copies of *yb*. The Newberry copy results when the unturned bottom *ya* sheets in a small separate pile are turned and placed on the heap during the comparatively short time that type in the xb^1 state is perfecting. If the inner forme were first corrected just before the uncorrected *ya*

the press) that the 'uncorrected' state of outer F had been proof-read and corrected before perfecting began. But since the book was set by formes from cast-off copy, the lack of such proof-reading in the 'uncorrected' outer forme can be only high possibility. Nevertheless, even in these circumstances the development of some mechanical basis for inference has a value not to be despised.

iii. *Unique Aberration*

(3) The phenomenon under examination must not be so narrow or unique as to introduce the possibility that a recognized printing procedure is not being revealed but instead that we are examining only an aberration—some human variation or failure that must be regarded as producing a sport.

An example of evidence too narrow might be the omission of a line or two in a reprint. Under certain conditions a critic might find there was an insufficiently broad base to decide whether the line was dropped inadvertently by eyeskip, or deliberately by a compositor setting by formes and pressed for space. If in the original two lines begin with the same word, and in a reprint the first line is omitted, it is a reasonable inference that eyeskip caused the omission. Unfortunately, not all such dropped lines can be so readily explained. No one can be quite sure whether in the one presently known variant forme of Q1 *Richard III* the omission of 1. i. 101–2 (*Bro.* What one my Lord? *Glo.* Her husband Knaue, wouldst thou betray me?) was inadvertent or mechanically inspired.

On the other hand, the possibility is always present that bibliographical evidence may reflect only some unique aberration. If a turned letter righted were the only variant in

sheets were exhausted, the Newberry sheet could result from the perfecting of the remaining *ya* sheets with the first corrected inner forme (*xb¹*). But then no explanation for the Hyde copy is possible, for any separate small pile of outer-forme sheets would need to be in state *yb*.

NOTE: Two presses printing inner and outer formes as white paper and then each perfecting for the other may be shown to be impossible for this book.

a forme, the narrow evidence might reflect press-correction, in which event the error will appear in the early pulls. But the order might be reversed: the correctly positioned letter could present the earlier state and the turned the later if the type had been jerked out by an ink-ball and carelessly replaced. Ordinarily no evidence could point to the cause and so determine whether plan or accident had produced the variant, and therefore what was the order.

An editor could be forgiven if he did not lie awake at night over this problem of a turned letter, but parallel examples will arise that require editorial decision. Indeed, a similar problem appears in Dekker's *Old Fortunatus*, although here it was fortunate that analogy within the quarto proved very helpful in broadening the base of the evidence and assisting the hypothesis that a regular printing procedure was involved, not just an accident.

In the eleven extant copies of the play only two press-variants occur: on sig. A4 the misprint '*Radienee*' was corrected to '*Radience*', and on sig. B1 the verb 'court' originally set with a capital 'C' was reduced to lower-case. Either *might* have been, in reverse, the effect of type pulled free by an ink-ball and carelessly repaired. Yet five copies of the quarto show the state with the error in both sheets, and only one copy is irregular in that the correct state of sheet A is bound with the error in sheet B. This similarity suggests that roughly the same time was taken in proof-reading each forme, and such evidence would encourage the probability that both press-variants were actual press-corrections, not random errors fortuitously perpetrated at about the same time in machining two different formes.[1] The probability is strengthened,

---

[1] It is much more probable, certainly, that the similarity in the number of copies of each forme machined with an error reflects an original mistake rectified by a normal printing operation than that there was fortuitous agreement in the time at which a piece of type was jerked out of two independent formes. One should note that uncorrected states of formes tend to cluster in the same copies, evidence that sheets were collated, and bound, in roughly the same order as they came off the drying battens.

moreover, by the critical inference that in a verb the reduction of a capital letter suitable only for the word as a noun would appear to represent a planned operation in sheet B. If so, the close analogy of the physical evidence suggests that planned alteration operated in sheet A as well.

It is sometimes objected that bibliographical analysis of textual problems starts from internal (that is, literary) evidence and therefore is impure.[1] Trifling as this example from *Old Fortunatus* may be, it has interesting implications. In the nature of the discipline, textual bibliography cannot always divorce itself from critical considerations. For instance, collation of all the known copies of *Old Fortunatus* disclosed only these two minor variants. But the presence of these variants revealed in any individual copy could never *by itself* furnish strictly bibliographical evidence about the order of the readings as printed.

Literary criticism, even though certainly at a very low level, is required to suggest that '*Radienee*' is a misprint and that the verbal symbol called for must be the other variant '*Radience*'. (If this were a variant in a Sanskrit text, none but a specialist in the language would know which was the misprint: a bibliographer could not determine from the evidence.) Correspondingly, whether a capital 'C' is more appropriate for a noun or for a verb is not a matter for bibliography to decide. Strict bibliography, moreover, is helpless to demonstrate the order of the variants in either of these sheets, taken separately. Some argument for a possibility can occasionally be advanced on general experience that when there is a marked disparity between the number of copies preserved of each state, the state with the small number of copies is likely to be the uncorrected. But in *Old Fortunatus* the evidence is a stand-off.[2] Observation of general printing practice might suggest that the confusion of lower-case *c* and *e* is a fairly

---

[1] Sir Walter Greg in *Review of English Studies*, N.S., vii (1956), 307.

[2] In the 11 extant copies, 5 contain the uncorrected state of A and 6 the uncorrected state of B.

common one in foul-case; but a devil's advocate could suggest that the error might then be readily *inserted* in the text if a careless repair were made of a loose type. Palaeographical experience (as in the manuscript of Dekker's *Welsh Embassador*) shows us that the usual *majuscule* form of the letter *c* might be used quite at random with the *minuscule* form in a manuscript when no intent to capitalize could be present. This argument is not so reversible as that for the confusion between *c* and *e* types, for a pressman plugging a hole left by a jerked type would scarcely be consulting manuscript. At best, one can say only that it is still possible for the pressman to have secured the repair type from the upper-case box if he had not seriously considered the sense.

The bibliographical interpretation of the physical evidence can suggest, at any rate, that each variant was made at about the same time in the machining of the respective formes. This does not bear on the order (because of the equal proportion of the two states) but it does lead one to infer that each was the result of a planned operation within the normal printing process and not a random aberration. If, then, from the bibliographical evidence we can infer conscious alteration, we can utilize our critical judgement (with a confidence not otherwise possible) to find the more obvious planned correction in the two examples. When this appears to be the change assumed to be from 'Court' to 'court', the whole argument is complete and it is possible to agree that both variants seem to be similar in their origin and thus in the order of their change.

To any sceptical observer the closeness of the above examination and the triviality of the result might well appear to be a supreme example of pedantry intolerably complicating a relatively simple decision. I should have full sympathy with this view if the value of the end here were seriously thought to justify the means. But at the moment we are looking at the means alone, and we must take our arguments where we find them as simple illustrations of principles, the more elementary the better. The nature of the evidence, and the kind of reasoning possible from it to arrive at conclusions of various degrees of certainty, is alone in question. Techniques learned from quite trivial problems may sometimes be used to solve those of considerable importance.[1]

IV. *Insufficient Evidence*

(4) Too small a number of preserved copies of a book may prevent the discovery of all the bibliographical evidence that might be present in an edition and thus may shackle the interpretation of its significance. Such a limitation may keep us (*a*) from making a just estimate of the evidence we have, (*b*) from developing supplementary evidence of the kind that can often be found from the examination of a large number of copies, or (*c*) from possessing all the evidence necessary for a sound conclusion.

(*a*) A case in point would be this. The only difference in a forme in the two preserved copies is a turned letter in a word making some sense in either variant, like *bands* or *bauds*. If either sense is possible, which is the turned and which the upright letter would be an important question; but here the bibliographer would be helpless to assist the critic since the priority of the two states would be uncertain. Without a knowledge of the order, one could only speculate whether the variant were an authentic press-correction or else a careless repair of a pulled type.

Even if many copies were available, only bare probability could be claimed for any argument that the isolated change was a press-correction because it was made very early in the run, or that it was more likely the faulty repair of a pulled type because it was made towards the end. Indeed, the very evidential basis for such interpretations based on the time of

---

[1] Moreover, if one is an old-spelling editor of *Fortunatus* one must decide whether to print 'Court' or 'court'. This is a practical problem, whatever its low importance to the literary critic, and an editor likes to have a reasoned, factual basis for judgement even when trifles are involved.

the alteration may be shaky, for we know from the facts gathered in the examination of Jaggard's First Folio that in some shops, at least, and for some books, at least, the sheets off the press were scanned from time to time for technical imperfections. Thus even though it might be somewhat abnormal, substantive press-correction could be made relatively late in the run as part of a regular operation.

However, uncertain as such evidence is, at least some grounds for conjecture—even though admittedly slight—would be afforded by the relative number of the two states preserved in a generous sampling of copies, whereas no conjectures are even possible if only a very few copies are extant.[1]

The first edition of *Sir Martin Mar-all* was published in 1668 without an author's name on the title-page. In 1691 the fourth edition added Dryden's name for the first time, but on a cancel title-leaf. For many years no copy with the original 1691 title was known, and I had examined twenty-five or more copies without finding one until in the summer of 1958 I came upon an example among some newly acquired plays at the University of Chicago, and more recently (I am happy to say) the Bodleian Library has secured a copy. The only textual difference between the two titles is that the cancellans adds the name that was wanting in the original. If one could be sure that these two were just about the lot, one could be tempted to conjecture that *possibly* the cancellation of the original took place before publication and that the known pair represent aberrant copies that were accidentally placed on sale without the cancellation. Yet another interpretation of the neutral evidence is almost equally plausible, for cancellation may have been decided on immediately after the edition had been placed on sale. On the other hand, if a number of copies with the original title turn up in the future, then we may be reasonably sure that the original form was issued by intention and that the cancellation occurred a

[1] See note B, p. 131.

sufficient time after publication to allow some quantity of the first issue to be sold before the second issue was prepared. We do not yet have enough copies of this edition generally available to make a firm and just decision.[1]

(*b*) A quarto begins and ends with a half-sheet, but in the final half-sheet the requisite number of running-titles is not present that would indicate that the fold had been printed either by single or by twin half-sheet imposition. In such an event the pattern of watermarks will be quite positive evidence for one or the other imposition provided enough copies are preserved to offer trustworthy statistics. If only a few copies are extant, the clash of watermarks would be more trustworthy as evidence for single half-sheet imposition than would be coincidence in the pattern for twin half-sheet imposition. That is, either a watermark in both half-sheets, or none, should ordinarily be positive evidence that the two half-sheets were independently imposed and machined. A single copy suffices to provide this information, and its trustworthiness can be doubted only by assessing the odds in favour of aberration.[2]

On the contrary, any single copy with a watermark in one half-sheet and none in the other can offer only negative evidence in favour of combined imposition of formes from each, for this pattern will fortuitously appear also in independently imposed and machined half-sheets. Only by building up evidence from a large enough number of copies, all with a consistent pattern, can negative be turned to

---

[1] See note C, p. 131.

[2] I have kept records of the watermark evidence in half-sheets of the many Restoration play quartos I have examined, and in my opinion this evidence is sound when a sufficient number of copies is examined. When the half-sheets were imposed separately, the inevitable clashes in the pattern begin to show up fairly soon. On the other hand, when twin half-sheet imposition has been the method, I can recall only one or two plays in which there has been contrary evidence, and this has been confined to a single copy or two. Whether these have been made-up, or whether some binding aberration has been responsible, I do not know. What I do know, however, is that the odds are vastly against the appearance of conflicting evidence in twin half-sheet imposition in plays of the sixteenth and seventeenth centuries.

positive evidence and neutrality grow to possibility, to probability, and finally to certainty. When only one or two
copies are preserved, consistency in the twin half-sheet
pattern cannot be relied on to be trustworthy as evidence.
With three or four copies, perhaps, a possibility appears.
Certainly by the time one reaches the ten preserved copies of
the 1609 *Troilus and Cressida* which have the cancel preliminary fold (printed with the final half-sheet M), high
probability if not certainty has been reached.

(*c*) Additional evidence affecting the soundness of conclusions may be revealed by the collation of a large number of
copies, whereas it may by chance be wanting when only a few
can be surveyed. The degree of certainty with which one can
view conclusions reached by such evidence is thereby
affected. Of seventeen copies of Dekker's *Satiromastix* (1602)
the uncorrected state of the inner forme of sheet B and the
uncorrected forme of outer F are known in only one example
each. In *The Magnificent Entertainment* (1604) only one
known copy contains the independently made second round
of proof-correction in outer H. It is of very considerable
interest to a critic that this round be separated from the later-
performed third round with which it would otherwise be
confused.

Among seventeen collated copies of *Westward Ho* (1607),
only one holds the uncorrected state each of inner E, outer F,
inner F, and outer G. In *Match Me in London* (1631) the
whole evidence that Dekker may have read proof for the
twin-imposed half-sheets A and L rests on only one observed
copy of the uncorrected state added to one copy of the first
round of the corrected state. The loss of either copy would
have destroyed the evidence for Dekker's intervention. In
this same play the uncorrected state of a forme is represented
by a single copy, versus twenty-five observed of the corrected
state, in outer B, outer D, inner D, and outer E. Especially
in this quarto an editor needs to know what were the
original readings set by the compositor, and what were the

proof-readers' unauthoritative alterations. Serious textual consequences could follow the editorial failure to isolate the alterations, here, of an almost wilfully sophisticating corrector.[1]

Textual critics have a habit of placing themselves in jeopardy by explaining anomalous readings as the result of proof-correction when evidence is wanting that the forme was ever corrected, or—even if it were—that the readings in question were produced by the corrector and not by the compositor in his original setting.

On sig. A4 of Dekker's *2 Honest Whore* (1630) some verse is set as prose. One of these pseudo-prose lines reads as follows:

old *Iacomo*, sonne to the *Florentine Iacomo*, a dog, that to meet profit, would . . . (1. i. 124–5).

In reconstructed verse the passage reads:

Hip. What was he whom he killed? Oh, his name's here;
Old *Iacomo*, sonne to the *Florentine*
Iacomo, a dog, that to meet profit,
Would to the very eyelids wade in blood
Of his owne children.

There is, of course, an outside chance that the reading is correct as it stands. But if there is corruption, the difficulty might be righted by placing a stop after *Florentine* to show that the repetition of the name applies to the same man and that only *Florentine* identifies his father; or else by transferring *old* from the son to the father. At any rate, one critic would like to transpose the word *old*; and to rationalize the decision he explains the origin of the error as follows: the compositor must have set the line initially in error with an

[1] Also in *Match Me* no accurate picture could be made of the structure of the heap of paper from which the outer forme of sheet F was perfected if either the single Newberry or the single Hyde copy had been unavailable; and indeed the usual order of perfecting, instead of the order with a special abnormality, would have been assumed quite automatically without the knowledge of both copies. See note A, pp. 130–1.

old before each *Iacomo*. Thereupon either the proof-reader marked the wrong one for deletion, or else the compositor mistook the marking and removed the wrong *old* after *Florentine* when he corrected the type from the marked proofs.[1]

This explanation is advanced without any satisfactory evidence that the forme was ever proof-corrected or that the preserved reading in the text was the corrector's responsibility and not the compositor's own setting from manuscript. The only suggestion that physical evidence exists for proof-correction is the statement that the spacing of the prose line is abnormally wide between several words, and that this anomaly shows that the word *old* has been removed from the line. Actually, this interpretation is put forward in terms of high probability if not certainty; but according to the standards advocated in these lectures it is wayward in its interpretation of evidence.[2] Even if the evidence had not been suspect, moreover, the hypothesis could not have ranked as more than simple possibility (if that) in the absence of further evidence from the collation of many more copies which might show (if this forme were indeed press-altered, although there is no evidence that it was) whether the line in question was affected by the proof-reading.[3]

Under the best of circumstances, in the absence of specific evidence one can advance only the barest possibility that an invariant reading is the press-corrector's rather than the compositor's, and especially—to add to the speculative element—that the compositor has misplaced the proof-correction ordered. When a hypothesis for original compositorial

---

[1] *Studies in Bibliography*, xiii (1960), 51–52.

[2] See below, pp. 124–6 for an analysis of the evidence.

[3] When editing the play I thought the reading was in error, and followed Hazelton Spencer in emending it by the transfer of *old*. This transposition seemed best to solve the difficulty of having Mathaeo kill in fair fight an old man who was son to a still living father of the same name. I conjectured that the compositor's memorial error or eyeskip was responsible for the error, even though this implied a correctly lined manuscript set as prose. (See *Dramatic Works of Thomas Dekker*, ii (1955), 219, textual note.) However, I have slowly come to believe that I was mistaken. I should now prefer the stop after *Florentine*.

error is as valid, in the state of the evidence, as a hypothesis for proof-alteration, it is dangerous to suggest that the natural explanation is less plausible than the unnatural one.

A tempting example occurs in the same play. The quarto reads:

> And fed vpon thee: good *Mat.* (if you please) so base as
> Scorne to spread wing amongst these. (11. i. 37–38)

Since the manifestly correct reading is

> Scorne to spread wing amongst so base as these

one might conjecture, on grounds similar to those alleged for the *old Iacomo* crux, that the compositor omitted *so base as,* that it was restored by the press-corrector, and that the compositor misplaced the phrase when correcting the type. Without doubt, such an explanation would fit the preserved evidence. But possibility is not probability, and a critic would be ill-advised to accept this hypothesis unless the actual two states of the quarto were discovered. The reason for caution is not far to seek, for an interlineation in the manuscript (perhaps above a deletion) could have been misunderstood by the compositor; and thus the error could easily have appeared in the original typesetting. If one objects that surely the proof-reader would have caught the mistake under these conditions, one is speculating further about the problematical actions of a problematical functionary. The preserved evidence does not suggest that this book was proof-read carefully for meaning.[1]

A simpler and therefore a better example may come on sig. C1 of *Match Me in London.* At 1. iv. 2 the quarto reads:

> It spake! not, did it?

[1] One reason most textual bibliographers would prefer to assign the error to the compositor's original typesetting is that the compositor's typesetting is not hypothetical, whereas the proof-reader's ministrations must remain hypothetical for any forme until collation discloses the evidence. Moreover, the keen concern for meaning manifested by the proof-reader of an early dramatic text is usually a figment of the critic's imagination.

Possibly this is mere compositorial confusion, and I should be inclined to put it down to transposition of the exclamation point were it not for the presence of the comma where the exclamation should have been. Thus since the uncorrected state of the outer forme of C has not been recovered (but ought to exist by analogy with other formes in this book set by formes from cast-off copy), in the interval one might conjecture that the misplaced exclamation mark was intended by the proof-reader to substitute for the comma after *not*. (We do know in this play that the proof-reader added eleven such exclamations among the press-variants that have already been recovered.) Just the same, nothing quite takes the place of evidence, such as we find on sig. F1 during the correction of outer F. Here at III. i. 54 the uncorrected state reads

To honour by it be secret and be wise.

In the corrected state a comma was added after *by*.

To honour by, it be secret and be wise.

Here, surely, we have a demonstrable case of misplacement of a proof-reader's correction, and it may give us some support, by analogy within the same book, for conjectures about such matters as the misplaced exclamation mark at I. iv. 2.

But the analogy is not exact enough to carry over to the two queried passages in *2 Honest Whore* (printed in another shop) in which the situation is very different. Because the principle is of some interest—that is, the advisability of imputing error to the press-corrector instead of to the compositor setting from manuscript—it will be worth while to examine a little more closely the evidence for the speculation about *old Iacomo*.

The hypothesis advanced with undue certainty was that the word *old* had been duplicated in the original typesetting and that the wide spacing of the prose line indicated that one *old* had been marked in the proof for excision and deleted, but by error the compositor had removed the wrong one. If we examine the recovered press-variants in this play, we find two each in three formes and a single variant in a fourth forme. Each correction concerns a literal or some obvious misprint, nothing that in any way resembles the attention to meaning that would be required for the corrector to have his attention caught by the repetition of *old*. This analogy from the same text, therefore, does not encourage the conjecture, which is now seen to be based on an appeal to general printing practice and not to the specific operations observed in the book under analysis.

But indeed the very evidence of wide spacing between words on which the whole conjecture is based proves to be suspect. A real question may exist whether the three slightly wide spaces between words in this line are extensive enough for the original typesetting to have admitted the four types required for *old* and its accompanying space. Moreover, the next line begins with the word *meet* that is manifestly too long to be included in the preceding line and yet cannot be broken between the two lines. The simplest, and most plausible, hypothesis is that the compositor was forced to adopt his slightly wide spacing merely to justify the original line.

When one pursues this obvious direction of inquiry and studies the compositor's work, one finds plenty of evidence to suggest that this simple explanation is the true one, for various other prose lines in the same forme indicate that the spacing of the line in question is by no means abnormal for this workman. On the very same page, for example, lines 9 and 12 have words just as widely separated as any in the *Iacomo* line, and it is particularly noteworthy that line 36 on the preceding page is spaced throughout perhaps even more widely than is this line. Since it would be patently absurd to infer that words have also been removed from these various lines (and others throughout the quarto) in the process of proof-correction, it is clear that the mechanical evidence adduced for disruption in the *old Iacomo* line is worthless, and certainly that its terms were improperly stated.

The conclusion is inescapable that far too much loose speculation of this sort is indulged in by critics who are properly eager to find a mechanical explanation for textual anomalies but whose sense of bibliographical reasoning is deficient in rigour. Critics have been particularly free in their treatment of evidence, or rather of non-evidence, in this matter of hypothesizing the interference of the press-corrector as evidence in favour of a certain form of emendation. When we do not know whether a forme was or was not proof-read,[1] we have a very infirm basis for conjecturing the proof-reader's interposition except in elementary and obvious examples as illustrated from *Match Me in London*.

It is dangerous to substitute ingenious speculation for ascertainable fact such as is involved in the collation of a sufficient number of copies that might recover some positive evidence for press-alteration. The danger is the more apparent in that such essentially idle guesses are thereupon utilized as evidence for the editorial choice of readings. If one takes it that the *Iacomo* lines are somehow corrupt, one has a choice of simple transposition under the influence of the repeated name, or else the possibility that only missing punctuation is involved at the end of the verse line, where it is often wanting in this compositor's work, and likely in the manuscript as well.[2]

---

[1] The automatic assumption is surely wrong that every forme of cheap commercial printing was necessarily proof-read. Any editor of Elizabethan play quartos is familiar with some formes in which the typographical errors are so gross as to make it seem impossible to suppose that these formes had been read. Dr. Hinman's findings about the relative carelessness of the proof-reading in the First Folio when 'trustworthy' compositors were setting as against the care expended to read the apprentice Compositor E's output is most suggestive.

[2] Few editors, perhaps, can be exempt from criticism about driving evidence too hard in the search for mechanical explanations of textual phenomena on which to base emendation. In selecting the transposed reading for my edition in this text I suggested that the manuscript was correctly lined and that the compositor's eye wandered between the two *Iacomo*s. This is a simpler theory than the one involving

But if one entertains oneself with if's and and's and suspects that quite conventional wide spacing conceals the removal of a word in some lost stage of press-correction, then the complexity of the circumstances flowers, guess is built upon guess, and an editorial decision is made on nonexistent or quite distorted evidence, all in the name of bibliography. It is small wonder that the discipline has sometimes got a bad name when guesses from false evidence masquerade in this manner as scholarship.

v. *Alternative Causes for Variation*

(5) Even when we can have some confidence that we have recovered the details of the mechanical operation, the interpretation of the physical evidence may admit more than one normal and plausible explanation. Often these explanations will differ in respect to the reasons for the operation, the agents who ordered or performed it, or else the time at which it was performed.

The cancel title-leaf of Dryden's *Sir Martin Mar-all* (1691) has been mentioned above and the point made that the examination of a score or more of copies is insufficient to allow for any certainty, or even probability, whether the two examples known at present with the original title represent binding error (perhaps before publication) or the regular first issue. However, the question is actually more complex, for a third plausible explanation can be drawn from the essentially neutral evidence: it might be argued that no copies were sold initially except with the cancel title, and that the two known copies with the original leaf are remainders, among the very last to be sold after exhaustion of a too small supply of cancel title-leaves. The interpretation of

the proof-reader, but it requires the assumption of an anomaly (the setting of verse as prose) without inquiring into the causes, or necessity, and this is faulty scholarship. However, the basis of the difficulty lay in the fact that I was deficient in critical acumen to take it that the father was also being named. No matter how else one may wish to emend, a strong stop after *Florentine* seems required.

the evidence might be completely reversible, in this manner. Hence when two or three such attested interpretations are possible, caution should rule in one's estimate of the degree of probability that may be accorded to any choice.[1]

Caution is especially necessary in the interpretation of mechanical evidence as error rather than as a product of normal procedure. Dover Wilson writes thus about the date on the title-page of Q2 *Hamlet* altered in press from 1604 to 1605: 'It should be remarked also that the two dates on the title-pages in no way indicate two different categories. All they imply is that the book was being printed about the turn of the year and that the compositor set up one date and the corrector preferred the other.'[2] No other interpretation is allowed for, yet it is clear that all books with press-altered dates cannot represent a conflict of opinion between the compositor and corrector. Whoever drew up the wording of the title-page presumably wrote in the date that would be placed in the imprint, and on the face of it one would suppose that the master rather than the compositor was charged with the important wording of the title whenever the publisher had not dictated its form.

But we do not need to appeal to general probability, for the considerable number of books with press-altered year of publication[3] indicates sufficiently the desire on the part of stationers to have copies for sale with an up-to-date imprint in the new year whenever publication occurred in November or December.[4] A clear-cut case for the alteration of a date to bridge sale over the end of a year is offered by Gervase Markham's *Second Booke of the English Husbandman*, which

---

[1] See note D, pp. 131–2.

[2] *The Manuscript of Shakespeare's Hamlet* (1934), i. 124.

[3] For a selection and discussion, see Bowers, *Principles of Bibliographical Description* (1949), pp. 51–55.

[4] That the pressure was strong to offer books to the public with a current date may be shown by the late-seventeenth-century newspaper advertisements of publication in November and December for books in which the imprint bears the date of the following year.

has a general title-page dated 1614 or 1615 by press-alteration. One of its parts, *Pleasures of Princes*, also contains the press-variant imprint date of 1614 and 1615. One would scarcely like to conjecture repeated conflict here between compositor and proof-reader.

Hence the attested parallels suggest that such press-altered dates were customarily planned from the start in order to provide copies for sale in the two states; and to infer otherwise is to assume unique error as against regularity in printing process. Yet the unusual can always appear, and lacking such confirmatory evidence for a set practice as is found in the Markham volume, and others, a critic might still wish to avoid the automatic assumption that in any given occurrence a planned change of date was inevitably more probable than a difference of opinion between the functionary responsible for the title-page imprint and the corrector. If a legitimate question can actually exist in an example like *Hamlet* Q2 (although I doubt that it can),[1] then neither interpretation can credit itself with more than a possibility.

Any theoretical equal balance between two hypotheses may be tipped in one direction or another by suggestive evidence; a critic may always take the responsibility for his convictions based on his individual assessment of the weight of the evidence. It would be as wrong in bibliography as it is undesirable in horse-racing to rule out differences of opinion.

For instance, it was a common practice for Restoration play quartos to be cast-off and the copy for the first half of the play to be printed on one press and that for the second half on another. When firm evidence is wanting for any given book, it perhaps will remain a difference of opinion whether these two presses were in the same shop (despite occasional typographical variation), or whether the work was farmed out between two printers for greater speed. The critic who favoured the two-shop hypothesis might query why Restoration compositors could not serve two presses

---

[1] See note E, p. 132.

machining alternate sheets, as is found in such Elizabethan quartos as *Hamlet* Q2, and why, instead, they chopped the book in two parts for typesetting. On the analogy of plays like *1 Honest Whore* (1604), which was divided by sheets between three or four shops, he might wish to generalize that a major division between parts of a play ought to indicate the apportionment of printing among different houses. And he could adduce some Restoration play quartos with alternate sheets printed by two presses to support his position.

On the other hand, a different critic might feel that Elizabethan analogies are inappropriate to the Restoration, that one method of printing was as fast as the other, and that the increase in the size of Restoration printing-shops and in their number of presses brought less need for expedients required of one-press Elizabethan printers to rush a book into print. The practice of divided copy for books is so wide-spread in Restoration play quartos, it might be argued, as fairly to cancel itself out if every printer took in his fellow's washing, so to speak. In multi-press shops there would seem to be no necessity to farm out parts of a small job like a play quarto; and indeed printers should have had too few presses for commercial operation if the speedy production of a play quarto could not be handled within one shop. Depending upon his convictions, any critic faced with such a problem (especially when the evidence has as yet been insufficiently investigated) may argue for provisional probability in favour of his case despite the weight of the other side's arguments. But if he does so, he should be aware of the dangers of his position. In such shadowy territory between the probable and the possible in bibliographical evidence, the conservative position inspires the greater confidence.

NOTES

Note A, p. 110. If either one of the Hyde or Newberry copies had not been observed—one out of twenty-five—the irregularity in the perfecting of the heap would not have been in evidence. It follows that the postulate of normality about the turning of the whole heap before perfecting could mislead a critic as to the relative number of copies printed of the uncorrected states of each forme. If the inner forme were first on the press, absence of the Newberry copy would make the evidence seem to demonstrate that fewer copies of the uncorrected outer forme had been machined than of the uncorrected inner, whereas the reverse would be true. Correspondingly, if the outer forme were first on the press, the absence of the Hyde copy would indicate that fewer copies of the uncorrected inner forme had been machined than of the uncorrected outer, whereas the reverse would be true. See Fig. 3 above.

Note B, p. 118. That conjectures based on such slight evidence are occasionally incorrect does not destroy the advantage that lies in playing the odds that they will be right. For what it is worth, my own experience in collating Elizabethan dramatic texts indicates ordinarily that formal press-correction is made early in the run. However, enough contrary examples are known to give one pause when the temptation arises to think of such conjectures in terms of firm probability. For instance, only 2 copies of outer C in Dekker's *Magnificent Entertainment* (1604) are known with a pair of indubitable press-corrections, whereas 14 copies contain the uncorrected state. In *If This Be Not a Good Play* (1612) 3 copies have the altered state of inner B as against 10 for the uncorrected state. In outer F only 1 copy preserves the corrected versus 12 exhibiting the uncorrected state. These are exceptions and much in the minority, but they effectively prohibit generalization at any level of certainty.

Note C, p. 119. Other possibilities will occur to any ingenious mind. It might be argued, for instance, that no copies with the original title were sold at first but only those with the cancelled state, and hence that copies with the cancellandum represent late remainders when supplies of the cancel leaf had run out. In rebuttal one might object that leaves intended for cancellation were generally torn as a warning to the binder and so the lack of any tear in the two known original title-leaves should be evidence that these two copies were bound at a time before cancellation had been decided on. Indeed, their pristine state may be a straw in the wind, even though we know very little about the process of mutilating a cancellandum leaf and how invariable it might be. When evidence is so uncertain, and the number of preserved copies so few, *possibility* is all that should be suggested for any offered solution.

Note D, p. 128. Unfortunately, we cannot be sure that a leaf intended for cancellation was invariably torn as a warning to the binder. Hence we cannot argue positively that the lack of any tear in the cancellandum in the two known copies is evidence that they were part of an authentic first issue. Their pristine state *might* be of some significance; on the other hand, it might indicate nothing about publisher's intention. If a leaf were intended for cancellation and the cancellans leaf had been machined before the printer collated the copies to arrange the sheets for the binder, we may suppose that the cancellandum usually would be slit. But if the sheets had been collated before the cancel was decided on, even though no sale had taken place, then it would seem that no agent might be concerned to tear the leaf intended for excision. This evidence, also, is neutral and reversible. The unslit cancellandum could mean true first issue, or accidentally issued early copies, or remainders. No one of these is inherently more probable than another, although general experience might lead a descriptive bibliographer (who must make *some* decision for the purpose of listing) to prefer the first two to the third.

Note E, p. 129. In cases like this, one may hesitate to cut the evidence too fine. That the change in the title-page of *Hamlet* Q2 was accompanied by textual press-correction in the O half-sheet printed with the preliminaries does not necessarily imply that at the same time the corrector altered the date because he thought it was wrong. We have no means of knowing whether a set number of copies with the 1604 date had not been ordered, and that the proof-corrections in signature O were not delayed until the time came to alter the date. For instance, when the title-page date of James I's *Essayes of a Prentise* was changed from 1584 to 1585, the misprint 'Edinbrugh' was simultaneously repaired; yet we cannot conjecture that it was the discovery of the misprint that caused the press to be stopped and hence that the alteration of the date was a mere afterthought. Nor need the alteration from 1589 to 1590 in the imprint of Lodge's *Scillaes Metamorphosis* have been a happy idea inspired by the unlocking of the forme to improve the typography of the title. The alternative —that the opportunity to make the title more pleasing to the eye was taken consequent upon the stopping of the press to alter the date—is just as plausible. Evidence such as is found in these examples is subject to no certain interpretation, and therefore under most circumstances probability must be denied to either side of the explanation.

V

THE INTERPRETATION OF EVIDENCE: THE POSSIBLE

1. *Abuses of Evidence*

A GREAT deal of bibliographical evidence as it is applied to textual phenomena can be interpreted on an isolated and individual basis to provide a satisfactory explanation. Yet such an explanation, even though it may appear to be plausible, cannot be rated as more than a possible one whenever the strength of the argument depends in some considerable part on an appeal to a general printing practice that does not seem to run counter to the slight evidence.

For instance, it is a keystone in the study of compositorial spelling characteristics to assume that the need to justify a line of prose (or a full line of verse) by tinkering with spaces and with spellings will sometimes affect the consistency of a compositor's spelling habits. Compositor B of the Shakespeare First Folio with marked regularity spells *do* as 'do', but Dr. Hinman observes that what is for B the anomalous long spelling 'doe' is noticeably more frequent in prose than in lines of verse that do not fill the measure. From this evidence he conjectures, it would seem correctly, that at least one of the causes of Compositor B's rare irregularity is the occasional addition of the final -*e* as a means of justifying a slightly short line.

Rigorously applied, and buttressed by sufficient evidence, this proposition might well be ranked as a *probable* one when considered in general.[1] But not all applications of a probable proposition are of equal validity: the precise application of

---

[1] The press-variants I have observed in Dekker's plays, for example, show more justification by altering the spelling than by narrowing or widening spaces.

a probable generality to a concrete case does not always make the result as probable as the theory. Thus in Compositor B's work if an anomalous *doe* spelling is found in a particular prose line, any supplementary evidence must be studied with caution before the automatic explanation is given that the long form was caused by his need to justify the line and did not result, say, from his following copy.[1] Indeed, even if the long form may be truly anomalous in verse, is its simple appearance in a prose line adequate evidence to appeal to justification instead of copy-influence in lines where no concrete evidence is available that there was a need to justify or that this specific method of justification was used?[2]

Obviously, it is a sound principle that every line needs justifying. What we do not know and ordinarily cannot tell when we face a well-spaced and balanced line is the exact method by which the compositor adjusted it. Did he estimate his need as he set a given line and was he expert enough to come out right in this particular instance? Or did he set the line and then as a separate operation did he increase or decrease its length? When all appears to be normal, and we have no observed anomalous spellings, we can scarcely know whether the compositor justified by altering the spaces between words, by tinkering with the spelling of one or more words, or by some combination of the two. We can seldom know whether the amount needed to expand or reduce in order to secure a balanced but tight line was sufficient to warrant the removal or the addition of even so much as a single letter instead of the minor adjustment of one or two relatively thin spaces between words.[3]

---

[1] See note A, pp. 156–7.

[2] To a limited extent, part of this question is answered in the latter part of the note above, but the text from this present point continues the examination in different terms.

[3] In discussing justification it is assumed that ordinarily when a line was not necessarily to be set out to the full measure, the compositor would justify it by adjusting spaces in the quads that made up his white in the right margin. If so, only a full line would call for spelling variation as a means of justification.

Just as obviously, we may sometimes see that lines have required extensive justification and that a particular method has been chiefly employed. The wide-spaced line in 2 *Honest Whore* containing the *Iacomo* crux, I should maintain, shows justification by increasing the spaces between several words well beyond normal when it became clear that the word *meet* (that now begins the next line) could neither be broken nor included entire. The opposite may be equally clear. When we see a line with unusually narrow spaces between words and an uncharacteristic use of abbreviations, we are warranted in conjecturing that reduction in the length of the line was needed for correct justification. In the Shakespeare First Folio, for example, the appearance of an ampersand is almost an automatic warning that adjustment has been made in an overcrowded line. Any editor of dramatic texts is accustomed to seeing speech-prefixes reduced in order to accommodate justification. If the usual form has been, say, *King.*, and abruptly one encounters *K.*, the line will almost certainly be a full one.

In either case, of course, we cannot ordinarily be sure that alteration of spelling did not accompany the use of other visible means of performing the mechanical operation.[1] It follows that our belief that spelling anomalies will often have a mechanical basis must in great part rest on our precise knowledge of an identified compositor's habits both in respect to the characteristic spelling of any word under examination and in respect to what can be determined about his ordinary method for justifying full lines, whether by spacing or by spelling alteration, or by both.

Hence when a question of copy-influence is involved, according to the circumstances one might believe that a given irregular spelling in a normally spaced full line had a simple mechanical explanation from the act of justification.

[1] On the evidence, some compositors would reject the wide spacing customary in 2 *Honest Whore* as an unsightly and sloppy procedure, and would expand spellings in preference to this marked spacing-out of words.

Thus one might make a general appeal to the printing process to argue for strong possibility or even probability. On the other hand, when not much information is available, or when the word is less fixed as an habitual spelling, one might be more cautious and require additional evidence before accepting such an appeal as valid in any individual case even as a useful possibility.

Certainly, in ordinary circumstances when the irregularity of the spelling is not fully established, the mere appearance in prose of a suspected anomaly can scarcely offer the concrete evidence that should always support bibliographical reasoning. Instead, the 'slight evidence' that I have remarked as necessary to support deduction ought to provide some positive indication that the line has been contracted or expanded in accord with the form of the spelling. Wanting such mechanical evidence to support the fragile assumption about the spelling, the argument might well be denied even the lowest level of possibility, for the results cannot be trusted or employed as evidence for further decision.[1]

It is difficult to over-emphasize this point, since the abuse of evidence is at the heart of much faulty bibliographical argument. When the only evidence is the anomaly in the text requiring explanation, and no supplementary mechanical evidence is present to direct the critic to the exact method of printing that produced the anomaly, only rarely may we say that a strictly bibliographical interpretation of the evidence is *possible*, even though we may know that the interpretation is not inconsistent with general printing procedure. Some concrete evidence in addition to the phenomenon to be explained is usually necessary. This is why appeals such as Dover Wilson makes to a hypothetical proof-reader altering

---

[1] This is far from denying (as remarked earlier) that spelling tests in dramatic quartos should remove from the statistical account all anomalous spellings in prose lines. This isolation is a mere precaution against the confusion of good and bad evidence in the evaluation of a general proposition. It bears no resemblance to the problem envisaged here, in which conjectures about the nature of the underlying printer's copy might derive from the evidence of a single example.

a hypothetical compositorial reading should leave us cold, and why they cannot be called, in all candour, a bibliographical argument despite the terms in which they are cast.

One must repeat again and again that not only is a possibility not a probability, but a theoretical possibility is not always an applied bibliographical possibility. This is not a sterile quibble but a lively issue, for texts may get themselves edited on principles that will scarcely stand a touch of daylight. Some years ago in his New Cambridge edition of the play Professor Dover Wilson very ingeniously adapted the suggestions of earlier critics to explain the massed entries in the Folio text of *The Merry Wives of Windsor* as the product of printer's copy made up by a scribe from a number of actors' parts.[1] Like so many other deductions in textual matters, this one yielded to a better method when a few years later Professor F. P. Wilson brilliantly showed in *The Library* by an inductive examination of the total evidence that the phenomena were in fact the personal characteristics of the scribe Ralph Crane, who frequently wrote out entries like this when copying a manuscript. Hence there was no reason to suppose that the entries in *The Merry Wives* reflected any peculiarity in the source of the manuscript used as printer's copy.

One might argue, if one chose, that since in pure theory a copy made up from players' parts *might* conceivably be organized by mass entries, we should still entertain the possibility that this was true for *The Merry Wives*; and indeed the Introduction to the Yale Folio facsimile has on some such grounds given fresh currency to this persistent error. (By similar logic the moon might still be made of green cheese.) But we may not take it that purely hypothetical reconstruction of a plausible situation means that

---

[1] A massed entry is the notation at the start of a scene of the entrance in a group of all the characters, although some will make their actual entrances later at different points in the scene. The true entrance will not be indicated, ordinarily.

the interpretation can therefore be called *possible* from any scholarly point of view, without concurring evidence.

In *The Merry Wives* there is no evidence of the sort to support the hypothesis for players' parts, but a great deal in favour of Ralph Crane as the scribe. Hence we have an illustration of the danger of constructing theories only on the evidence of the phenomenon to be explained and immediately with full circularity, taking it that the possibility of a theory shows that the theory itself is possible! An editor's position in respect to the characteristics of the Folio text of *The Merry Wives* would differ materially according as he accepted Jaggard's copy as one drawn from players' parts or as the product of Ralph Crane's scribal pen. And since editorial policy ought to be based on some theory about copy, an editor might well be concerned not to be the dupe of pseudo-bibliographical argument in such an important matter.[1]

11. *Neutral Evidence*

The distinction between a possible hypothesis and a possible application is of especial moment when—as often happens—more than one possibility can be envisaged and no one interpretation seems manifestly superior to the others. Evidence susceptible of more than one equally plausible interpretation may be called *neutral* evidence. Unless a critic can strengthen one or other side of the argument by supplementary evidence of some sort, it is clearly dangerous to attempt to treat an interpretation of neutral evidence as furnishing a possibility serious enough to govern a decision. Neutral evidence of this sort is a bibliographical commonplace, and it provides the happy hunting-ground for all the critics who know least about bibliography and its laws of evidence, and who therefore have fewest inhibitions about speculating in pseudo-bibliographical terms.

Evidence is also violated too frequently when, in fact, interpretations are not equally plausible, and a critic, unaware

[1] See note B, p. 157.

of the technical weakness of his case, confuses the hypothetical possibility with the bibliographical possibility—one that requires sterner tests before application.

We may revert for a moment to the sample case of Mr. Musgrove's arguments that editors should choose the First Folio press-corrected reading *sentences* in *King Lear*, i. i. 170, instead of the Quarto and the uncorrected Folio reading *sentence*.[1] Because he cannot conceive of any grounds except reference to copy that could persuade the proof-reader to alter the singular to the plural, he hypothesizes not only the press-corrector's reading against copy but also reference to copy in a distinctly unusual manner for which there is no evidence other than the theory itself based on the internal nature of the crux in question. There is nothing in Mr. Musgrove's complicated theory for the origin and correction of the assumed error that is not hypothetically possible in the limited sense that it is a physical possibility. But one ought to require more rigorous conditions than this form of possibility before an application can be ventured that will satisfy scholarly standards. These conditions are wanting.

Indeed, internal analogy usefully puts any editorial advocate of the plural *sentences* in a difficult position. There are two other variants in this page with *sentences*, but neither by the widest stretch of imagination could suggest reference to copy. Moreover, just the same situation holds on sig. rr2 in the fourteenth line of the first column. Here the Quarto copy has 'hot bloud in', a phrase that was presumably among the errors altered in the Folio printer's copy, since in the uncorrected state of the Folio page the line reads 'Why the hot-blooded *France*, that dowerleſſe tooke', altered in press by the proof-reader to 'hot-bloodied'.

Reference to copy is difficult to establish here on critical or linguistic grounds, and there are no other evidences in the forme for consultation of copy by the press-corrector.

[1] See above, pp. 86–87.

True, if one were rationalizing the error a complex argument might be developed that would involve the corrector misreading the annotated quarto, taking it that the imperfectly deleted 'i' of 'in' in Q 'Why the hot bloud in *France*, that dowerles' ought to be part of the word, and scrupulously restoring it. This is hypothetically possible, but no editor (one hopes) would without further evidence take it as bibliographically so possible a theory as to warrant his assuming that the proof change was made from reference to copy.

Indeed, it would seem that *hot-bloodied* is no more arbitrary a change than *sentences*, and that the proof-reader (if the same) who on his own responsibility was capable of making the one might well be as capable of making the other on the same terms. There is no more bibliographical (or critical) reason for us to accept *sentences* as an authoritative reading derived from copy than *hot-bloodied*. Is it not thoroughly unreasonable to ask editors to choose readings that violate critical intelligence, as these do, merely because a theoretical explanation for the change can be contrived in terms of the printing process? Hypothetical possibility does not by itself create that bibliographical possibility that may legitimately contribute to editorial decision.

Neutral evidence is invariably insufficient evidence on which to base any assumptions requiring decision or the formation of hypotheses that could ultimately influence decision. Whether the exemplar of Q6 of *1 Henry IV* that served as printer's copy for the Folio was read against the company's prompt-book is a matter of some importance in connexion with the Folio's variant readings. Hence Dr. McManaway was on the soundest of grounds in protesting as an insufficient basis for hypothesis Dover Wilson's one small piece of evidence that can be interpreted in two ways: 'Because F [McManaway writes] reads "President" at ii. iv. 32, where Q has "present", Wilson insists that Q6 (1613) . . . must have been collated with the prompt-book, but the emendation is required by the context and is hardly beyond the powers of whoever purged the text of oaths.'[1]

Improper bibliographical arguments are sometimes made from neutral evidence on the analogy of what-might-have-been instead of on the basis of facts that indicate what was. Time and again the incredibly slight evidence for the copy-text of the Folio *Richard III* drove Mr. Walton in desperation to unsubstantiated hypotheses from neutral, even from negative evidence. For example, he offers as significant a list of fourteen occurrences of place-names set in roman in Compositor A's section of F *Richard III*.[2] In each instance the name is set in roman in Q3 but in italic in Q6, and Mr. Walton argues from this and from a list of eleven territorial titles in which the same conditions obtain that

> It is reasonable to suppose that Compositor A in setting up his part of the F text of *Richard III* would follow his normal practice and put in italics the majority of proper names, even though they were not italicized in his copy, but that in a number of cases he would, if there were only comparatively few proper names italicized in his copy, fail to follow his normal practice. It is easier to accept this supposition than the supposition that compositor A failed on all the occasions listed above to follow his normal practice despite the fact that the form in his copy was in accordance with it.[3]

There is no need to discuss here the details of the faulty basis in facts represented by this argument,[4] except to remark that the primary assumptions are wrong. Mr. Walton to the contrary, Compositor A's normal practice in English history plays, as shown in the three parts of *Henry VI*, was not to italicize place-names, or territorial titles when preceded by 'of' as in the formula 'my Lord of Yorke'. In *Richard III* the facts are quite simply these. Compositor A nowhere italicizes any place-name. He italicizes only two

[1] *Shakespeare Survey*, i (1948), 128.
[2] J. K. Walton, *The Copy for the Folio Text of Richard III* (1955), p. 65.
[3] Ibid., p. 66.
[4] An extended consideration will be found in 'The Copy for the Folio *Richard III*', *Shakespeare Quarterly*, x (1959), 541-4.

territorial titles in the formula that he ordinarily sets in roman: one of these (IV. i. 14 'my young Sonne of *Yorke*') was present neither in Q3 nor in Q6 and therefore can have no bearing on the printed copy-text; and the other (IV. iv. 472 'What Heire of *Yorke* is there aliue'), though roman in Q3 and italic in Q6, would argue against Mr. Walton's case for Q3 were it not that *Yorke* is here quite clearly used as a personal name that Compositor A would invariably italicize, as in 'great *Yorkes* heire' in the very next line.

Stripped of its faulty information, therefore, Mr. Walton's argument could be corrected to run thus: in the two respects given, Compositor A had a certain fixed method of setting names in roman, a practice that coincides with the fixed method of Q3. Since Q6 italicizes these names on an equally fixed basis, we should expect Compositor A to slip up once in a while and set a few names in italic if Q6 had been the copy-text. Since his roman setting is invariable in *Richard III*, we must as a consequence assume that Q3 was the printed copy he set from, for no slip-ups occur.

Stated in this bald manner, the case is patently absurd. It asks us to accept as positive evidence Compositor A's failure to do what only as a hypothesis he might have done. This is distorting neutral evidence with a vengeance.

Luckily, not all critics attempt to strain neutral evidence so severely. More understandable, and one may hope more typical, examples concern interpretation of such evidence in quite plausible and sound, but unfortunately in divergent, ways. For instance, one commentator thought that the late Philip Williams would have strengthened his case for the twin half-sheet printing of the Q *Troilus and Cressida* cancel fold in the same formes as the final half-sheet if he had insisted that 'the decision to insert the cancel was made almost as soon as printing began, for otherwise the type of the original title-page would almost certainly have been distributed as soon as sheet A had been perfected'.[1]

---

[1] *Shakespeare Survey*, 4 (1951), 162.

This is unexceptionable reasoning, but it may err in its estimate of probability, or rather of near certainty—a dangerous phrase on such evidence. We do not have any information whether at this time a title in the first-printed sheet would ordinarily be kept standing as a matter of policy until the book was finished. If, as likely, the title would be distributed at leisure, it would be perfectly possible for the title to remain standing for the whole length of the printing provided that the types were not required for some other purpose in the shop. That a compositor actively working on a book distributed as little as possible of the miscellaneous type that was not in general use may perhaps be suggested by the manner in which, for instance, several pages of italic type in the text of Thomas Randolph's *Aristippus* (1630) were left standing for a minimum of three or four days instead of being distributed normally with the roman in the same formes.[1] Moreover, the possibility that advertisement title-pages would be run off for posting might also contribute to the preservation of the title in standing type. Finally, not all initial play quarto sheets containing text as well as title-page and preliminaries were set or machined first.[2]

Thus it can be only a matter of opinion (at least at present) whether any given printer would or would not for any given book keep a title in type either by plan or by circumstance: it is *not* an ascertainable bibliographical fact in general printing practice, or for this particular book. It would seem that the evidence of the standing type in the title of *Troilus and Cressida* is quite neutral in so far as it may bear on the question of when the cancel was decided. The cancel *might*

---

[1] 'Marriot's Two Editions of Randolph's *Aristippus*', *The Library*, 4th ser., xx (1939), 163–6. Italic type is also kept standing under abnormal circumstances in Dekker's *Magnificent Entertainment* (1604), but there the explanation seems to be the desire not to reset Latin text in a planned second edition.

[2] Dr. Robert K. Turner, Jr., has recently demonstrated beyond any doubt that the first sheet of Q1 of *Midsummer Night's Dream*, with the text starting on sig. A2, was last composed and printed. See 'Printing Methods and Textual Problems in *A Midsummer Night's Dream* Q1,' *Studies in Bibliography*, xv (1962), 34–35.

have been ordered a few minutes after the first forme of sheet B was put to press; it *might* have been decided as late as the last full sheet L. Under these circumstances it may be that Dr. Williams was well advised not to use such an 'iffy' interpretation among the better-supported pieces of evidence at his disposal.

III. *Conflicting Evidence*

Neutral evidence impartially suggests the possibility of several more or less equally plausible explanations. Conflicting evidence is more complex, since parts of it suggest one possible conclusion and other parts suggest the opposite. To take an example, a serious textual problem revolves on the contamination of texts by memorial transmission and the isolation of such characteristics of this memorial contamination as may assist an editor to recognize it whether alone or in conjunction with alternative readings from a partly authoritative source. The nearer one of these so-called 'bad-quarto' texts comes in its influence on the printing of an authoritative text, the more concern a critic must feel to understand its nature in every possible detail.

The latest textual investigations of *Romeo and Juliet* have reduced the influence of the bad First Quarto on the good Second Quarto to quite negligible proportions and to that extent have returned the problem of the bad quarto from the hands of the editors of the play to the general textual critics.[1] But *King Lear* is another matter, and here the intimate connexion of the bad quarto with the printer's copy for the Folio texts makes editing an impossibility on other than subjective and critical terms unless the editor has contrived relatively firm hypotheses about (*a*) the formation and authority of the Quarto text; (*b*) the construction of the printer's copy for the

---

[1] P. L. Cantrell and G. W. Williams, 'The Printing of the Second Quarto of *Romeo and Juliet* (1599)', and Richard Hosley, 'Quarto Copy for Q2 *Romeo and Juliet*', *Studies in Bibliography*, ix (1957), 107–28, 129–31. See also *Textual and Literary Criticism* (1959), pp. 86–89 for a summary, and p. 30, note A, above, for further remarks.

Folio from this Quarto text and some other document; and (c) the Folio compositors' treatment of this printer's copy.

These three points are arranged in an ascending order of susceptibility to bibliographical treatment, the last being most subject to mechanical solution. Dr. Hinman has recently identified Compositor E's work in F *King Lear* and thus has provided the basis for an accurate estimate of the characteristics of Compositors B and E in *King Lear* as compared with E's characteristics elsewhere in control texts like *Titus Andronicus* and *Romeo and Juliet*. Hence for the first time a firm bibliographical base has been prepared for an editor to arrive at some estimates of the amount and kind of compositorial error in each page and from this data to isolate more clearly the work of the annotator of the Folio printer's copy. But, beforehand, compositorial analysis must move into the second category by settling on mechanical grounds whether the printed quarto text used by the annotator was Q1 exclusively, or, as has been suggested without any systematic analysis, pages from Q2 as well.[1]

When this task has been performed in a definitive manner, then we shall have all the facts that bear on the amount of annotation that was made in the printed copy-text. So far mechanical analysis can prevail in future examination of the problem, but other techniques will be necessary to decide from the factually tested evidence what was the nature of the manuscript used for consultation by the annotator. Moreover, to some extent the answer to the question of the faithfulness of this annotator will lie in the answer to the first question—the formation and authority of the basic Q text.

Here we enter into a problem that I touch only in relation to this discussion of evidence, for no certain solution may ever be found. On the one hand we have critics who believe Q *King Lear* to be a text memorially reconstructed throughout. That a play text could be cobbled up largely by the memorial

---

[1] A. S. Cairncross, 'The Quartos and the Folio Text of *King Lear*', *Review of English Studies*, N.S., vi (1955), 252–8.

reconstruction of a minor actor has been amply shown in G. I. Duthie's study of Q1 *Hamlet*. But this classic pattern emphasizing very good reconstruction of a reporter's own speeches and of the scenes in which he participated, and very poor elsewhere, is not found in such a seemingly reported text as Q *Richard III*. Here a variant hypothesis has been contrived—that the company itself reconstructed the play from their collective memories when on tour and wanting a prompt-book. Plausible as is this interpretation of the evidence as applied to *Richard III*, it is a bucket that can be carried to the well only so often. Hence critics of *Romeo and Juliet* Q1 have strained the evidence unmercifully to avoid the duplication of the *Richard III* hypothesis and to discover a reporting actor, even in the most improbable figure of Romeo.[1]

But not even this feeble recourse is available for *King Lear*, and the opening question strikes at the heart of the Quarto's authority by inquiring whether the text is an 'official' or 'unofficial' memorial reconstruction. One dogged school has maintained against all critical evidence that the Quarto represents an authorial first draft. The latest hypothesis comes from Dr. Walker, who tries to find a middle ground between the two. In brief, she envisages a set of Shakespearian 'foul papers' as the basis, but one actor dictating from these papers to a very naïve scribe. From time to time this dictating actor elects to recite from his faulty memory not only his own part but other parts in the scene instead of reading from the manuscript before him.

This omnibus hypothesis combines all plausible explanations that have been offered,[2] but whether the conflicting

---

[1] Improbable, I take it, because one would not expect this to be a part acted by a hired man, and a shareholder would scarcely pirate his own company's play to a provincial company.

[2] '*King Lear*—The 1608 Quarto', *Modern Language Review*, xlvii (1952), 376–8, and *Textual Problems of the First Folio* (1953), pp. 41 ff. A recent article has offered still another: damage to the bottom of the leaves of a foul-papers manuscript. See J. S. G. Bolton, 'Wear and Tear as Factors in the Textual History of the Quarto Version of *King Lear*', *Shakespeare Quarterly*, xi (1960), 427–38. See also *Shakespeare*

evidence is actually resolved in a manner that can be trusted to guide editorial decision is open to question. Not all anomalies are explained by any means, for whenever an attempt like this is made to raise the authority of the Quarto, a corresponding down-grading of the Folio must be made. And when the Quarto is exalted, no satisfactory suggestions account for what would need to be the wilful divergence of the annotator from the Quarto (and presumably also from his manuscript) in passage after passage, nor can these numerous variants be accounted for in the lost manuscript that was collated.

In such a situation when evidence is so amazingly in conflict, and when various opposing possibilities can be suggested by the different facets of the evidence, pending a resolution that may never be accomplished the poor devil of an editor is torn between the dangers of critical eclecticism that would end in the simultaneous approval of all theories or else the narrowing and even distorting effect of provisionally following one possibility to the exclusion of any other. It is true that mechanical evidence can provide an editor with some firm ground amidst these cross-currents, in so far as this evidence relates to the bibliographical connexion of the Folio and Quarto. But for the more advanced reaches of speculation about this text, the evidence is conflicting, and the rigorous following of any one hypothesis seems to produce textual results that do not always equate with critical approval. In this position, until or unless more certainty is won, the wise course may be to take the conflict of evidence as a warning signal against too narrow an editorial theory.

That it is dangerous to ignore literary criticism in the application of what may be only a bibliographical possibility is shown by Sir Walter Greg's shrewd remark about those

---

Quarterly, vii (1956), 177–82, for the hypothesis applied to other plays. As the writer remarks, his hypothesis (like Dr. Walker's) is an attempt to combine some reconstruction with a basis in the actual foul papers. The presentation of the evidence is not so systematic as to be convincing, however.

editors of *2 Henry IV* who believed that the Folio text was set from a manuscript but whose choice of variants was more consistent with the theory that the Folio derived from an annotated quarto. This proposition has been illustrated more recently in *Romeo and Juliet*, where—if there were no other grounds for suspicion—Dover Wilson's theories about the extensive annotation of Q1 as copy for many parts of Q2 would come in question because the editorial practice enforced by his (superior) critical taste runs exactly counter to the logic of his (erroneous) bibliographical position.

iv. *Criticism and Bibliography: the Interpretation of Evidence*

From this survey several points emerge. Not all bibliographical evidence can be so conclusively interpreted as to lead to demonstrable conclusions. Indeed, it is ignorant and dangerous to assume that bibliographical analysis and demonstrable results are always to be equated. Sometimes bibliographical analysis can construct an explanation that is absolutely and irrevocably certain. Sometimes it can provide a working hypothesis that by scholarly requirements is sufficiently certain to serve as a basis for editorial theory, or one that is highly probable, or probable enough to influence editorial decision; or one that is an excellent possibility, or barely possible, or is not strong enough—either because of the lack of evidence, or the conflict of evidence, or else its neutrality—to permit any weight to be given it except as mere speculation.

In many problems when bibliographical analysis cannot offer demonstrable results, the critical judgement must be welcomed in assessing the complex of evidence. Indeed, the more a bibliographical interpretation approaches the speculative, the more reliance should be placed on the critical judgement as a brake on technical guess-work, which is—after all—not a great deal better than any other kind. That *sentences* in *King Lear* by any literary standard would seem to be inferior to *sentence* should have been a warning flag against an attempt to justify the inferior reading by speculation clothed in bibliographical terms.

Correspondingly, when larger bibliographical reconstructions depend upon a linked series of hypothetical and somewhat unnatural circumstances, the critical if not the comic spirit may well be justified in viewing them with a more than ordinary reserve.

Now that we know that compositors are often not nearly such dreadful corrupters of immortal words as we once were told, pressure develops to explain textual contamination as coming from some other source, even though the scapegoat may be a much less convenient one. In some plays the memorial-reconstruction of an actor, plus some working-over, as with Q1 *Hamlet*, offers a very satisfactory hypothesis with a considerable amount of positive evidence in its favour. Other plays with something of the same stigmata want such specific evidence of agency, or else may present better texts than might be supposed to proceed from such a narrow memorial origin. The book-keeper is now growing in fashion as a corrupting agent, either a book-keeper who reconstructs whole plays from memory, or—more popularly—one who trusts to his memory more than to a manuscript before him when he is making a copy of a play.

If my own memory serves, the most common Elizabethan references to actors requiring prompting apply to the prologues, surely a special case where a faulty recollection would have little in context to support it. For the rest, the minute attention assumed to have been given by the Elizabethan book-keeper to the text he is prompting is, I think, problematical indeed.

The annotation in extant prompt-books shows that book-keepers had to get actors on to the stage on cue and that they had to prepare properties for use. These activities would interfere with a close word-for-word prompting. Moreover, under Elizabethan repertory conditions it would presumably be impossible for actors to recite their lines in the verbatim manner required in the present day.[1] It is possible, indeed, that Q1 *King Lear* or Q1 *Richard III* represents on the whole a fair approximation of what the audience heard any afternoon at the Globe. Under these conditions, the ability of an actor to extemporize must have been remarkable, and, as a matter of fact, the various bad quartos show how actors' memories brought in clichés, reminiscences of other plays, and what not, to piece out their memories. It is unlikely that modern conditions serve as any reliable parallel to Elizabethan, or that a modern actor, who may be left almost speechless by a memorial lapse, bears any resemblance to his differently trained Elizabethan ancestor.

Whatever evidence we have may suggest that the times when an Elizabethan actor would need prompting were few, given his ability to invent, and they would be chiefly concerned with getting on to some particular piece of necessary business. Under the repertory system, therefore, the bookkeeper's close attention to the text could not be like the scrupulous word-for-word operation performed by the modern prompter, who is also instructed to correct (privately) departures from a fixed text that is rigidly enforced.[2]

Modern scholars might well be sceptical of speculative theories that a Shakespearian book-keeper's recollection of any play would be as good as the actors', or even that he could have the sort of memory of a play that would take over in his copying of the text with the result that more variation might be expected from his transcription than from that of an ordinary scribe. Certainly, to found a complex textual

---

[1] See note C, p. 157.

[2] Even more of an ivory-tower concept is the occasional contamination supposed to derive from a prompter's noticing some actor's memorial lapse that seemed to him superior to the author's original in the manuscript before him. Whipping out his goose-quill, the book-keeper writes the lucky hit in the prompt-copy, presumably alters the actor's part, and attempts to have the (often quite minor) variant thereafter reproduced as an integral part of the performance. Actor's gag creeping into prompt-copy cannot be a possibility to be entertained with any seriousness; but naïve critics still advance it although no extant prompt-book affords any evidence of the practice.

theory affecting one's editorial judgement on hypotheses about the unknown capacities of an Elizabethan book-keeper is to be audacious indeed. And it would seem that the example of Dr. McManaway's common-sense analysis of Dr. Walker's views about the transmission of the text of *Hamlet* strikes a balance that is sometimes neglected in the *furor poeticus* of textual speculation:

Before agreeing, we must remind ourselves that there is no historical evidence whatever that the *Hamlet* prompt-book needed replacement; then we must decide whether to allow three staggering assumptions: (1) that if the old prompt-book were replaced by a new one the scribe would go to the trouble of assembling and copying out the players' parts instead of transcribing the tattered original; (2) that these players' parts had been modified (by the actors?) so as to include gags and other debasements; and (3) that the book-keeper would prefer and write down his own recollections of what had been spoken on the stage rather than follow his copy, thus introducing 'the anticipations, recollections and interpolations which require explanation in the F. text'.[1]

On the other hand, the more probable the bibliographical evidence in support of an interpretation, the more the impersonal judgement of bibliographical scholarship is to be preferred to personal judgement, at least in respect to limiting the operation of that judgement. That is, the mechanical interpretation of analytical bibliography, based on physical fact, when properly employed may ordinarily prove to be more trustworthy than the interpretation of the critical judgement from internal values.[2]

This validity of method founded on the inductive treatment of physical fact may spread over a wide range. It may operate on a very small point, such as offering some reasons for retaining the Folio's uncorrected reading *hot-blooded* in *King Lear* instead of what appears to be the proof-reader's

---

[1] *Shakespeare Survey*, 6 (1953), 167.

[2] Certainly its inductive method is more trustworthy than the deductions—the attempts to pluck out of thin air a theory that will fit most uncommonly recalcitrant pieces of evidence—that characterize present-day speculative Shakespearian textual scholarship.

aberrant *hot-bloodied*. It may decide that one leaf rather than the other of Nathaniel Lee's *Princess of Cleve* (1689) was intended for cancellation, and thus that the authoritative form of the text should be one version and not another.[1] It can ascertain what typesetting of each recto and verso of two versions of a cancel leaf in Congreve's *Double Dealer* (1694) is the primary authority for establishing the corrected text,[2] and which of the early gatherings of John Banks's *Cyrus the Great* (1696) are the original and which the reprinted and unauthoritative leaves with variant readings that can be automatically ignored.[3] It can ascertain that signs of disruption in the text of Thomas Southerne's *Disappointment* (1684) have a purely mechanical origin, and are unrelated to any peculiarities of content; and thus the deduction is wrong that censorship caused the removal of a scene.[4]

Admittedly, bibliographical investigation is more positive in its results than criticism when dealing with matters like these that are clearly mechanical. Physical evidence can positively identify beyond all question the order of the two 1669 editions of Dryden's *Wild Gallant*. Physical evidence can demonstrate that if more than one quarto of *Richard III* were used as copy for the Folio, the requirements of two simultaneously composing typesetters had nothing to do with the matter. Physical evidence almost wholly divorced from a reliance on meaning can establish that the beginning of Act III and the end of Act V in *Richard III* were set in the Folio from unannotated pages of Q3.

Physical evidence can have an important bearing on editorial treatment of a reading in iv. iii. 536 of *Richard III*, and—beyond that—on the possible use of Q6 as copy-text, at least in some part. In the Folio, lines 533–6 appear as follows:

---

[1] *Harvard Library Bulletin*, iv (1950), 409–11.
[2] *Papers of the Bibliographical Society of America*, xliii (1949), 191–5.
[3] *Studies in Bibliography*, iv (1951), 174–83.
[4] *The Library*, 5th ser., v (1950), 140–9.

> *Cat.* My liege, the Duke of Buckingham is taken,
> That is the best newes: that the Earle of Richmond
> Is with a mighty power Landed at Milford,
> Is colder Newes, but yet they must be told.

Line 536 had read in Q1, and in Q3 that must have been the Folio copy if Q6 were not:

> Is colder tidings, yet they must be told.

Q5 (1612) first substituted *news* for *tidings*, and Q6 followed its Q5 copy, of course, both without the Folio's metrically required but sophisticated addition *but*:

> Is colder Newes, yet they must be told. (Q5–6)

Mr. Walton, who is concerned to explain away this Q6–F concurrence, urges (p. 26) that *news* may have been the pure reading from the manuscript and therefore Q3 copy *tidings* was altered by the Folio annotator to *news*. Q1 *tidings* (repeated by Q3) he suggests may have originated as an actor's memorial recollection of iv. i. 37:

> Despightfull tidings, O vnpleasing newes.

That Q5 by accident stumbled upon what was the correct reading all along merely shows the long arm of coincidence.

Yet if one accepts Patrick's hypothesis for the communal memorial recovery of the Quarto *Richard III* text, a certain difficulty may be felt in believing that a recollection of a rather ordinary line spoken by Anne in iv. i would affect the reading of a line delivered by Catesby towards the end of iv. iii. On the other hand, if in the commonly accepted speculative manner one were to search for a mechanical explanation and to conjecture that line 534 *That is the best newes* independently contaminated the Folio compositor's memory in line 536 (while setting from Q3) as it manifestly had the Q5 compositor's, then strictly bibliographical evidence should provide a dash of cold water.

Line 534 containing *That is the best newes* (the conjectural contaminating factor) is the last line of Folio sig. s6ʳ, a page set completely by Compositor A. Line *535* begins sig. s6ᵛ, a page set wholly by Compositor B, and line *536*, containing *Is colder Newes*, is, of course its second line set by B. In the normal course B would have started to set where his copy was marked, with the first line beginning *Is with a mighty power*, and would have had no occasion to read the preceding line that had already been set by A. We cannot prove that his eye did not fall on this line, despite the marking in the copy that indicated he was to begin with the succeeding line; and if he did so we cannot prove that the word *news* (which he had no occasion to memorize since he was not setting the line) did not make so powerful an impression on him that it subsequently affected his memorial reproduction of *tidings* found two lines down in his Q3 copy.

This is all hypothetically possible, just as it is hypothetically possible that Q5 did not originate the substitution of *news* for *tidings* but instead (along with the Folio) copied the reading *news* from an uncorrected forme of Q3 not now preserved.[1] But if such acts of faith are to substitute for scholarship, it is well to notice at least that the bibliographical fact that the F compositors changed between the two readings quite alters the ease with which duplicate memorial corruption could otherwise have been conjectured. Given this physical fact, and its normal implications, something more of a hurdle must be jumped here if we are to believe in Q3 copy at this point (instead of the natural assumption that F merely followed Q6) than Mr. Walton permits us to see.

Physical evidence from identified types can establish the number of compositors who set the First Folio and the precise pages, and even part-columns, for which each was responsible. Physical evidence that composition was simultaneous from different type-cases enabled Dr. Hinman to demon-

---

[1] I hasten to add that this hypothesis about the independent derivation of *news* in Q5 and F from a lost state of Q3 has never been suggested, and I trust it never will be. I invent it merely as an exercise in hypothetical possibility: it is not intended to be taken seriously.

strate that Compositors E and B joined in setting *King Lear*
(and part of *Othello* and *Hamlet*) without our exercising our
critical judgement on the difficult evidence of the spelling
characteristics that separate these two workmen. Physical
evidence seems to assign various anomalies in the text of
Pericles to the characteristics of the compositors who
divided this quarto between them.[1]

These things can be proved, and they are the proper subject of bibliography applied to problems of text.

Except that transmission of a text is concerned, one might
be tempted to question whether inquiries into the lost stages
of the text, and the agents who affected it, before the print
was made are truly bibliographical. It must be admitted,
certainly, that most studies have not used the bibliographical
method, even though some reference to bibliographical
language may have appeared. Yet a bibliographical basis for
such an inquiry may be found in an analysis of the compo-
sitor(s) to estimate what in the printed text may be compositorial characteristics as distinct from those that may be
recovered from the underlying lost printer's copy.[2] The
matter is indeed of such importance for textual criticism as
to merit the closest handling. When Dover Wilson can
estimate that some 150 wrong readings exist in the Folio
text of *Hamlet* that might have passed muster as authoritative if Q2 had not existed, one can see the crucial need for
the most careful analysis of the nature of the copy behind any
Shakespeare play.

However, when bibliography in its pure state *can* operate
at the level of demonstration, and bibliography and critical
judgement clash (as in the cases of *The Wild Gallant*, *Cyrus
the Great*, and *Troilus and Cressida*), the critic must accept the

[1] Philip Edwards, 'An Approach to the Problem of *Pericles*', *Shakespeare Survey*,
5 (1952), 25–49.
[2] The investigation of the Dekker–Massinger *Virgin Martyr* or of *Lust's Dominion*,
mentioned above on pp. 13–14, 51, and 9–11, may be taken as an example. That
of F *Othello* below is another.

bibliographical findings and somehow come to terms with them. Critical assumptions by their nature can never be so valid in questions of fact as bibliographical evidence logically interpreted and applied. Indeed, this is not a question of degree: when a clash develops, strict bibliography must always be accepted as provisionally right, since step by step it rests on the impersonal inductive interpretation of physical facts according to rigorous laws of evidence. And, correspondingly, criticism must be provisionally wrong, since its interpretation of evidence can usually rest only on deductive opinion and comparative estimates of values. This is the lesson that bibliography has to teach; and it is valid provided the bibliographical analysis is firmly based and interpreted always within its own laws of evidence.

NOTES

Note A, p. 134. It is true that a spelling that is anomalous in verse should be equally so in prose in so far as there are reasons for it other than justification. This is no academic question, for many attempts to inquire into the nature of the underlying copy for a Shakespeare text rest on the assumption that an uncharacteristic spelling derives from the copy. Justification will certainly interfere with this assumption. Moreover, we can occasionally see in a reprint that a compositor will desert his copy in favour of an uncharacteristic spelling when no reason whatever is apparent. For instance, Compositor E of the First Folio, after an initial indifference, hardens to a distinct preference for the short form *do*. In his *Romeo and Juliet* stint he reproduces 44 short forms from his copy, changes 19 long to short, and follows his copy in spelling *doe* only 13 times. Nevertheless, once—and for no apparent reason—he changed his copy *do* to *doe* in a short verse line. In his *Troilus and Cressida* stint he follows *do* 9 times, alters *doe* to *do* twice, but changes copy *do* to *doe* once—although this occurs in a prose passage and therefore might be explained as the result of justifying the line. Nevertheless, we can never be certain that such an isolated reading has a mechanical and rational explanation—justification—because it occurs in prose, when we have encountered a similar aberration in a short line of verse in *Romeo and Juliet*. My argument for uncertainty is valid, I think, when particular weight must be placed on a relatively few pieces of evidence, and when our knowledge of the compositor's habits is less than perfect. I do not have the statistics, but I understand that Dr. Hinman believes that Compositor B is almost invariable in his use of the short *do* (his most firmly characteristic spelling) except when the line is such as to require justification. Correspondingly, if we had not known the copy for Folio *Romeo and Juliet*, but were guessing about its characteristics from our knowledge of E's habitual practice at this point in his career, we should have identified correctly the 13 *doe* spellings in his copy, but would have made one mistake with the odd *do–doe*. Here, of course, the single error would not have been critical since so much other evidence was adduced.

Note B, p. 138. A practical example in this play is furnished by C. J. Sisson (*New Readings in Shakespeare*, i (1956), 66), who argues for the original reading at I. iii. 31 'a minutes rest' instead of the frequent emendation 'a minims rest', or 'a minim-rest'. Sisson writes, 'Here Folio and Quarto agree, and it is difficult to assume that both compositors without collusion made the same improbable misprint of *minutes* for *minims*. . . .' *Collusion* is fantastical, of course; on the other hand, the reading in the Folio cannot be shown to derive from the use of Q as copy. Thus Sisson feels that independent compositorial error in misreading the same word in the two different manuscripts is an impossibility. This would be a first-rate argument if it did not ignore the question of the transmission of the text. If Q is a memorially reconstructed 'bad quarto', as seems likely, its reading derives ultimately from the prompt-book. If the copy for the Folio also derives ultimately from the prompt-book, as I believe, then F and Q could both print the same error if the source of the error were the prompt-book. Thus Sisson's argument collapses. And if (pseudo-bibliographical evidence aside) *minim* must be right, as I believe, on the close parallel in *Romeo and Juliet* and the simple evidence of the sense, then indeed the prompt-book origin of the Folio text is necessarily indicated.

Note C, p. 150. A look in Henslowe at the startling number of plays acted over the course of several months should be sufficient to disabuse us of any notion that an Elizabethan actor could possibly be letter-perfect in a part, given the many plays he had to keep in his mind, perhaps with no more than a rehearsal on the morning of the production. Neither the modern repertory company in residence, with a fresh play each week, nor a travelling repertory like that of Sir Ben Greet with a comparatively modest number of plays in active production, can even approximate Elizabethan conditions, which must often have required a strong infusion of something approaching the *commedia dell'arte* to make tolerable the extraordinary demands upon the memory. The close attention—in the modern manner—paid to the text by the Elizabethan book-keeper in the course of a play's production is, I suspect, pure fiction. And that he had much opportunity, or need, to know his texts so well that he could reproduce them memorially in any quasi-satisfactory way is, I have little doubt, even more of a fiction.

VI

THE COPY FOR THE FOLIO *OTHELLO*

1. *Printer's Copy: Problems in the Transmission of Texts*

AMONG the various serious problems of Shakespearian texts, none is more baffling than the group of plays printed in a version altered in the Folio from the form in which they had appeared in quarto. These plays divide into two main categories. In the first come those like *The Merry Wives of Windsor*, *Henry V*, and *King Lear* that were first published in what are technically known as 'bad quartos'. These texts seem to have no transcriptional links with any Shakespeare autograph manuscripts; instead, they appear to be the product of memorial reconstruction, the exact (and probably variable) nature of which is still in some doubt. Without much question such plays in their bad-quarto versions represent the maimed and deformed texts mentioned in the Preface to the Folio, and it was clearly of considerable importance to the Folio 'editors' that these texts should be offered in an authoritative corrected version.

In the second group come *Troilus and Cressida*, *2 Henry IV*, *Othello*, and *Hamlet* that had been issued in quartos printed from manuscripts that appear to have had a transcriptional link with the Shakespeare autograph, or to have been an autograph itself of some stage of the text. To this extent such quartos are authoritative for their texts. But it must have seemed to the Folio editors that the company owned manuscripts of a superior version. Copyright troubles may just possibly have enforced the use of a revised text for *Troilus and Cressida* as Sir Walter Greg suggested, although the matter is not demonstrable;[1] but for the rest there is no

---

[1] *The Shakespeare Folio* (1955), pp. 445–9 and references. Greg's arguments are very persuasive, but the need to assign different reasons for *Troilus* from those

hint of external difficulty. It is possible that a conscientious literary purpose was behind the Folio printing of these good texts revised by comparison with manuscripts different in their tradition from those that had served as copy for the quartos.[1]

For each play the central critical problem is to reach some conclusions about the nature of the manuscript behind the Folio text and of its relation to the manuscript from which the quarto had been printed. Strict bibliographical method does not touch upon this problem except as the establishment of the exact physical forms in print, and the recovery of what can be learned about the physical characteristics of the printer's copy, may provide some evidence to assist or to limit critical conjecture.[2] Nevertheless, although the literary relationship of the quarto and Folio texts is essentially a critical problem, the question of the physical relationship of the two prints lies within the province of bibliography. Although a corrected text from a bad quarto like *The Merry Wives of Windsor* appears to have been printed in the Folio directly from a manuscript, the printer's copy for other plays, like *King Lear* from a 'bad' quarto and *Troilus and Cressida* from a 'good' quarto, has been established as a quarto interlined or annotated marginally, and doubtless by inserted slips, with altered readings drawn from collation of the print against some manuscript.

---

obtaining for *Othello, Hamlet,* and *2 Henry IV*, for instance, may give one pause. It may be, after all, that the delay in printing *Troilus* and coming to an agreement about its copyright merely gave the opportunity for an alteration of the printer's copy that had not originally been contemplated.

[1] See note A, pp. 197–8.

[2] To take an extreme case, unless the bibliographer could provide evidence that they all could not be compositorial, the source of the prissy expansions of the colloquialisms made in the Folio *2 Henry IV* text might remain in doubt. But when, from our knowledge of the typesetters involved, we can offer this evidence, the critic is free to choose between the hypothesis (*a*) that they were present in the manuscript copy used by the annotator, or (*b*) that they were made on the initiative of the annotator. If the copy-text for the Folio were assumed to be a manuscript and not an annotated quarto, for 'annotator' merely substitute 'scribe'.

The general bibliographical problem is, first, to demonstrate whether or not the Folio text derived from an annotated quarto; and, second (if such a transmission can be established and if there is more than one prior quarto) to decide which quarto edition was employed and whether it was the copy throughout, or whether leaves from some other quarto might have been used to supplement the basic edition employed for annotation.

The correction of a printed edition to bring it into general conformity with a manuscript was a recognized Elizabethan method of providing a printer with copy, as may be seen in the revised second quarto of Beaumont and Fletcher's *Philaster* and *Maid's Tragedy*, each set from an exemplar of the first quarto corrected by reference to a superior manuscript. That even extraordinarily heavy revision could be handled in this manner is illustrated by Ben Jonson's own use of the quarto of *Every Man in his Humour* in preparing the much-altered Folio version. Quite naturally, the question has arisen whether the annotation of a printed quarto was a device by the theatrical company to keep an irreplaceable manuscript from the dangers of the printer's shop. If a company had sold a revised text to a stationer, it has been argued, the theatrical owners might find that the correction of an already existing printed exemplar by comparison with their manuscript was a quicker and cheaper way of providing copy for the printer than the commissioning of a whole new scribal transcript, such as—on the evidence—was made by Ralph Crane for *The Two Gentlemen of Verona*, *The Merry Wives of Windsor*, and *The Winter's Tale*.

On the other hand, at least some of the manuscripts used for the collation do not show any clear signs that they were prompt-books. If, then, a non-theatrical manuscript such as an author's 'foul papers', or some approximation of them, were used for the comparison of the print, two oddities appear that cast doubt on the preparation of the printer's copy in the theatre. It is unusual to find that a theatrical scribe had not collated from a prompt-book, which would be the most legible copy and the one that the company would regard as having the greatest authority.[1] Also, if another manuscript were in the company's possession, it is odd that this was not sent to the printer to serve as his copy, and be done with it. Any objection would seem unrealistic that the company would be concerned to provide the printer with the most desirable kind of copy from the printer's own point of view, and that they would go to the trouble and expense of puzzling over foul papers, say, to make up an annotated quarto for the sole purpose of saving the printer the labour of setting from a difficult manuscript.[2] These considerations have led various critics to believe that at least some annotated quartos were made up in the printer's own shop from the manuscript the company had furnished him as copy. In other words, the printer himself felt that it was easier and more economical to send even heavily corrected printed copy to his compositors than to have them set direct from manuscript.

The complexion of the case is quite altered if this theory is right, and it would seem that in some part it certainly is right. The Folio *Richard III*, and even Q2 *Romeo and Juliet*, may be too inferential to serve as an example, but a certain illustration is Roberts's consultation (though not annotation) of printed Q1 to assist in the typesetting of Act I of Q2 *Hamlet*. Inevitably, so long as the annotation was supposed to have been made in the theatre, critics could hypothesize some contamination from the theatrical agent's memory of the play (especially if he were the book-keeper) to explain why sometimes manifestly inferior readings appear to have been

[1] We must not confuse modern textual sensibility with Elizabethan. There is every indication that a theatrical company regarded its prompt-copies as the last word in authority, and indeed—for Elizabethan theatrical purposes—they were, though not for modern textual criticism.

[2] We may recall such manifestly foul manuscripts as that behind Q2 *Hamlet* given to the printer instead of clean scribal transcripts.

transferred from a generally superior manuscript. But if the alteration were done in the printer's shop, this avenue of critical escape is closed, and editor (and critic) must presumably deal with a much more naïve transcript in the manuscript portions of the text. It may be that in some circumstances the theatre would make up such a revised quarto from its prompt-book, but that in others the printer would independently take advantage of an earlier edition to ease his labours when the theatre had sent him its spare manuscript.[1] By and large the distinction is a critical problem not susceptible of bibliographical solution even though it is of interest to the textual bibliographer concerned to estimate what corruption in the print came direct from copy and what from the compositor.

However, it is the bibliographer's proper function to confine himself to the relationship that can be established, or inferred to exist, between physical documents. Thus the bibliographer can claim to settle the question whether an annotated quarto or a manuscript was the printer's copy; and if a corrected print of some earlier edition, whether this printer's copy was homogeneous or consisted—for convenience—of leaves from more than one exemplar, perhaps by chance of two editions.[2]

In determining the genetic relationship of texts, criticism relies almost exclusively on the study of variant substantive readings according to the principle that identity of reading implies identity of origin. Under most conditions found in a series of reprints[3] (I am speaking now only of printed books),

---

[1] See Note B, p. 198.

[2] I do not mean that two different copies of the same edition could ordinarily be distinguished. The reference is to leaves from two different editions such as Dr. Cairncross has guessed made up the copy for the Folio *King Lear*.

[3] The major condition in which simple readings are likely to fail as demonstrable evidence comes if one must distinguish the original from an immediately derived reprint when external evidence about their chronological order is wanting or is ambiguous. The falsely dated Pavier Quartos tripped up the Old Cambridge editors. A modern example is the evidence for the true first edition of Dryden's *Wild Gallant*: see above, p. 49.

the normal progress of corruption[1] in successive typesettings offers quite enough evidence from which to determine the derivation and order, even in moderately complex circumstances of mixed copy.[2]

On the contrary, when some correcting agent interferes with the text—like the collator charged with bringing a print into conformity with a manuscript of different textual tradition—substantive readings may prove to be unsatisfactory evidence. The normal reprint transmission of variants is disrupted by the annotator's correction of error and by the alteration or revision of seemingly satisfactory readings. This smoothing-out of the evidence on which textual criticism normally operates may occur in two different circumstances, each with its separate problems.

In the first, the original text has been reprinted at least once before the revision. In such a situation, if no interference had appeared with the normal course of reprint transmission, one's decision about the copy-text would rely on such evidence as whether the later editions had copied some of the unique variants of an earlier printing. The principle is firm that when error can be traced to some link in the process of transmission, and the error is repeated in a subsequent edition, this later text must derive (at least ultimately) from the intermediate edition.

Thus if a variant first appears in Edition B and is repeated in Edition C, the inference follows that C derives immediately from B and not from A. One proviso is that the variant is not of the sort that could be supposed to arise

---

[1] Correction is less frequently of use, for any edition can usually make the same correction independently, and thus the appearance of the identical correction is not necessarily proof of a genetic relationship. On the other hand, miscorrection may be fruitful evidence of relationship, especially if the basic miscorrection is further altered and rationalized in the text under consideration.

[2] Examples are Sir Walter Greg's demonstration that Q5 of *Richard III* was set from a mixture of Q3 and Q4 leaves, *The Library*, 4th ser., xvii (1936–7), 88–97; and James Steck's that Q8 (1694) of Dryden's *Indian Emperour* derives from a mixture of Q6 and Q7 according to the two compositors.

independently in both B and C, each using A as its copy-text. Almost any individual reading is susceptible of such an explanation, and usually there is no way of truly demonstrating the contrary.[1] Indeed, so variable are some forms in any text that a certain number of fortuitous independent agreements are to be expected. Whether C follows A but not B in such a reading as *these* versus *those*, in *gentleman* versus *gentlemen*, in *speaks* versus *speaketh*, is of no account as evidence in any individual case. Some words are constantly shifting back and forth in reprints; other changes of no significance may result from the similarity of compositors' linguistic habits. Obviously if C is dated in 1659, B in 1641, and A in 1599, many forms of C would agree with those of B even if A were indubitably its copy-text.[2] Sometimes quite astonishing random hits may be scored, as in the independent concurrence of the Folio *Richard III* with Q1–2 in the error *hop'st* instead of Q3–6 corrected *holp'st* (IV. iv. 45), or the independent agreement of F and the later Q7 at I. i. 168 in *smoothing word* for Q1–6 *soothing word*.[3]

What gives one caution in assessing as positive evidence any such individual shared aberrance is the thought that whatever forces operated on one compositor to produce the variant might on occasion also affect another compositor in a similar manner. The independent memorial contamination of one phrase by another may be explained readily, and experience with reprints shows how easily some words like *the* and *thy* exchange with considerable frequency. That the immediate cause of the shared error cannot always be

---

[1] Once in a while bibliographical evidence can encourage or discourage a particular view, as in the variant *tidings–news* in *Richard III* (see above, pp. 152–4).

[2] As another example, the general concurrence of F with the accidentals of Q2 *King Lear* as against Q1 does not necessarily demonstrate Folio derivation from Q2. Instead, we must consider that Compositor B set Q2 and was reprinting himself in part of the Folio text. When he was not typesetting, the apprentice Compositor E was operating, and his habits were in many respects similar to those of B.

[3] See also such common errors as F and the later Q2 *Othello* in *over* for *overt* at I. iii. 107; F and Q8 *Richard III* in *he* for *to* at I. i. 100; Q4 and F *Romeo and Juliet* in *else in* for *else is* at II. vi. 23.

determined indicates only that the stimuli are often obscure that produced similar reactions in the operation of two men's minds.

Another proviso is that the critic should not take seriously an agreement of any two editions in the correction of error when independence of action may easily be inferred. Thus concurrence of F and Q3 *Richard III* in *balme* instead of in Q5–6 *blame* (I. ii. 13) can scarcely be used as evidence, since *balme* is manifestly correct. F might have followed Q3 copy in *balme*, but it might as readily have corrected *blame* if Q6 had been the copy-text.[1]

In such circumstances a textual critic learns to weigh the significance of his evidence. One agreement in simple error may mean nothing, but fifty agreements (excluding modernizations) ought to be decisive, providing, of course, there are not thirty or forty on the other side. With selected though unslanted evidence, a point should be reached at which our common-sense view of probability rebels at being asked to accept any more coincidence as the result of mere chance. How much resistance a critic can put up before capitulating is very much an individual matter. Sir Walter Greg accepted Mr. Walton's case for the Q3 copy-text of F *Richard III* as self-evident; but Professor Alexander differs: 'This simplification [he writes] depends, however, on a notion of what Mr. Walton calls "indifferent variants" that runs counter to the principle that identity of reading implies identity of origin. The only exceptions to the principle must be accidental coincidences, and Mr. Walton asks us to accept more readings in Q6 as the "more or less unwitting discovery of the right reading" by the compositor of that reprint than our sense of probability can readily admit.'[2]

---

[1] That Q6 followed Q5 and failed to correct the error *blame* is no argument that F would have reproduced the reading if Q6 had been the copy. (It is a special case that in *Richard III* the annotator might also have corrected the error if Q6 had been the copy.)

[2] *Review of English Studies* ,N.S., ix (1958), 69–70.

In most cases of straight reprints, fortunately, the evidence is overwhelming, on the positive side, since the divergences of some intermediate edition from its source are almost certain to be followed, in the main, by its successors. The case is altered when (in the second category) the late edition under examination derives from the original edition or some other early print that is not an immediate predecessor. Here the force of the evidence turns from the positive to the negative. The agreement of the edition with any individual positive divergence is no longer in question except as an accidental factor to be sifted out.[1] Instead, the failure of the late edition to follow in general the unique divergences of any one of its ancestors is taken as grounds for ruling out such an ancestral edition as copy-text. Thus chiefly on negative evidence that variants are *not* repeated as one would anticipate, the critic can reduce the competitors to two editions only, and then revert to positive evidence to decide between these two final alternatives.[2]

When only two touching editions are in question, it is probably true that in some situations the derivation of the second from the first instead of from a manuscript may be almost impossible to demonstrate from verbal readings alone. The only proof, indeed, rests in positive evidence for the transmission of error from one to the other. Here a distinction must be made, for literary error may go back to a common source and may therefore have nothing to do with any case for the direct derivation of one print from the other.[3] For example, *pious bonds* shared at i. iii. 130 by Q2 and F *Hamlet* has been variously argued as the correct reading, as evidence that F was set from the Q2 error, and as a common error independently deriving from an ambiguously written original.

---

[1] See note C, pp. 198–9.

[2] See note D, p. 199.

[3] As in the common error drawn from the prompt-book by unrelated Q1 and F *Merry Wives of Windsor* in 'minutes rest' for 'minim's rest' (or minim-rest)—although the original has been defended.

It follows that the more mechanical the error and the less likely to have a literary origin, the more critics are inclined to give it superior weight. Thus Sir Walter Greg brilliantly demonstrated the dependence of F *King Lear* on Q's different states of press-variants, and press-variants alone would have been sufficient to indicate the correct order of the two 1669 editions of Dryden's *Wild Gallant*. The strongest evidence that some 160 lines begining Act III of *Richard III* are unquestionably printed in F from Q3 is the appearance in F of the mechanical repetition unique to Q3 of *as as* in the line at III. i. 123:

> I would that I might thanke you as as you call me.

No opportunity can exist in a case like this to argue for common origin of error in some other document instead of immediate derivation; nor could one conjecture that Q3 and F independently fell at this precise spot into the identical dittography, nor that the repetition was the right reading that Q3 and F had independently stumbled on— all these being the excuses ordinarily avouched for such identity of readings.

This reading also illustrates another method that may be used by textual critics to show derivation. This is the alteration of a reading that in a case of divergence could reasonably have come only from one and not from the other exemplar. In the illustration above, the Folio's Compositor A obviously was troubled by the repetition, but he preferred to retain it, though adding commas, rather than to take a chance on correction by dropping a superfluous *as*; and so the Folio reads:

> I would that I might thanke you as, as, you call me.

That the simple mechanical stutter of Q3 is being rationalized is an inevitable conclusion. One would scarcely like to argue that the F compositor independently made the same dittographical error as the Q3 workman, and then in a lost stage of proof-correction the proof-reader inserted the commas as somehow adding to the sense.[1]

Correspondingly, at III. v. 66 Q6 misprinted Q1–5 *cause* as *ease*, a reading that makes nonsense. The compositor of Q7 thought that he recognized the common foul-case confusion of *c* and *e*, and quite naturally he 'corrected' *ease* to *case*, thus establishing that Q7 was set from Q6. None the less, how difficult it is to deal even with such mechanical errors when they have some possible literary basis (as *as as* did not) may be shown by Mr. Walton's surely desperate argument that the Folio reading *case* did not originate in a similar independent rationalization of Q6 *ease* but instead was the F compositor's alternative and acceptable doublet form of the *cause* found in his Q3 copy.

When meaning is concerned, an argument can often be evolved that would defend either side. The more mechanical the evidence, or the more clearly the final reading must have developed from one of the two variants but most improbably from the other,[2] the less subject to exception is the evidence. Yet even at its most mechanical, some very odd fortuitous hits may occur to warn a critic against over-rash assumptions on too narrowly based evidence. For instance, the misprint *witchraft* for *witchcraft*, though readily explicable, is so far from inevitable that one might venture very long odds indeed against its coincidence in the same spot in two unrelated reprints; yet it is shared quite independently by Q4 and F2 *Hamlet* at I. v. 43, and so is *misheathed* independently by Q5 and F *Romeo and Juliet* at v. iii. 204, in error for *missheath'd*.

The problem of demonstrating whether a Folio Shakespeare text was set from a manuscript or from an annotated quarto when verbal readings constitute the only evidence is

---

[1] Or, that the proof-reader marked a comma to be added after *you*, and an *as* to be excised, and Compositor A misunderstood him and added commas after each *as*.

[2] As in the *cause–ease–case* sequence for F as against *cause–cause–case*. This latter is one of the readings that Professor Alexander believes violate our sense of probability when an argument is derived that Q3 was nevertheless the copy throughout. See above, p. 165, n. 2.

immensely complicated by the smoothing-out results of the annotation. When, as in *Othello*, only one quarto was printed before the Folio, or when, as in *Hamlet*, the first 'good' edition of Q2 and not a later one must have been the copy if a revised print were used, the errors in the printed copy-text are fewer, and the transfer of any manifest verbal error from Quarto to Folio is materially decreased through the correction of faulty printed readings by the collation with the manuscript. Hence only from scribal carelessness could any substantive error originated in the printing of the Quarto be carried over to the Folio to prove that the Q print must have been the basic copy. (Moreover, the manifest verbal errors of the Q compositor that would most clearly fall in this category are the very ones apt to call themselves most prominently to the collator's attention.) Those that elude his vigilance and are inadvertently passed are likely to be plausible enough to be argued for as no errors at all,[1] or else (since they are often close in their respective forms)[2] as error independently derived from a common original.

Against this line of defence there is no crushing rebuttal except the sheer weight of the quantitative evidence. But in the nature of the case, the quantity of transmitted verbal error about which there can be little difference of opinion has always been materially reduced by the normal operations of the annotator. In fact, in modern times every Shakespeare Folio text for which critics have suggested annotated-quarto copy has been in dispute whenever the first edition of a 'good' quarto is the only one that could have been corrected.

---

[1] The determination of error is certainly a serious problem, and there is little doubt that a number of wrong readings could slip by the annotator's attention, as we know from *Richard III* when F reproduces a variant that exists in Q2–6 but not in Q1. However, when the only check is critical suspicion, demonstration that the passed-on reading is corrupt is very difficult. For instance, were it not for the Q1 reading *vast*, it is likely that *dead wast and middle of the night* shared by Q2 and F *Hamlet* (I. ii. 198) would never have been questioned.

[2] Like *pith* (Q2) or *pitch* (F) *of merit* in *Hamlet*, I. iii. 22. It is a critical axiom that closeness of form like this marks error in one element, not revision.

Troilus and Cressida, Othello, Hamlet, and *2 Henry IV* are texts in which substantive readings alone have failed to settle the question authoritatively.

When in such examples as *Troilus and Cressida* the decision in favour of printed copy has received universal assent, the crucial evidence came not from the verbal readings but from the forms of the accidentals—specifically, in *Troilus and Cressida*, the variable lengths of speech-prefixes and the variable practice of setting names in italic or in roman, wherein the Folio repeated the Quarto's irregularities so faithfully as to go far beyond any possible suggestion of mere chance or of independent derivation from a common source.[1] These were details that the particular annotator of the copy-text for the Folio did not bother with, and fortunately the Folio compositors were on strange ground with classical names and so followed copy more conservatively than they did when reprinting English history plays, in which their fixed habits almost entirely removed such evidence as abounds in *Troilus and Cressida*.

Mechanical details from the printing process settled the problem of *Troilus and Cressida*. In a similar manner, mechanical details had long before settled that the Folio text of *King Lear* derived from printed copy. Here the transmission of forms that were press-variants served to isolate in quite mechanical fashion certain readings in the Folio that demonstrably originated with the compositor or the proofreader of the First Quarto and could not have derived in the Folio from manuscript copy.[2]

On the evidence, if the remaining problems in this category are to be solved in a manner permitting general acceptance, the mechanical or bibliographical method that

---

[1] In this illustration one need not depend upon the mere quantity of evidence. These shared features of Q and F *Troilus and Cressida* are so mechanical in the nature of their variation (i.e., so dependent upon the printing process for their origin) as to make any argument absurd that independent derivation from a manuscript could have created them in an identical manner.

[2] W. W. Greg, *The Variants in the First Quarto of* 'King Lear' (1940).

succeeded in *Troilus and Cressida* and *King Lear* is the only hope, for the normal textual-critical reliance on substantive readings has manifestly failed under the abnormal conditions fostered by annotated copy. At present, *Hamlet* and *2 Henry IV* appear to be very seriously snarled in controversy, whereas the proponents of manuscript copy for F *Othello* are silent under Sir Walter Greg's approval of Dr. Walker's annotated-quarto hypothesis. Yet Dr. Walker's case (though correct) is not nearly so copious or rigorous in its evidence as to make for an acceptable demonstration, and the application of another range of mechanical evidence is needed to supplement its narrow base.

11. *The Example of Richard III*

The peculiar problem of these plays is the identification of features of the Folio text reproducing features in the Quarto that must have resulted from the printing process. If the annotator slipped and failed to alter a corrupt Quarto reading, no way exists for us to know that this reading in the Folio (if indeed recognizable as corrupt) was produced in the Quarto by the printing process when the situation is one in which the shared reading can be defended on literary grounds or else assigned as error in a common source.

On the other hand, when as in *Richard III* the Folio copy-text must have been some quarto later than the first edition, enough unauthoritative variants that crept into the text in its transmission did in fact escape the annotator so that we may identify at least some of the characteristics deriving from the printing process that were transmitted. As a consequence, since 1885 there has been no doubt that the Folio text as a whole was based on a corrected quarto, and the only modern controversy has concerned the identification of this quarto either as Q3 of 1602, which contributed two extensive unannotated passages in Acts III and V, or as Q6 of 1622, or perhaps as both according to some exigency of annotation if a scissors-and-paste job were done.

Again it may be said that substantive readings have failed
to settle the complex matter, for the heavy blanket of correction has destroyed in large measure the readings from which
exact conclusions may be drawn. By the process of elimina-
tion from negative evidence one can decide with tolerable
certainty that (among the extant editions) the basic quarto
must have been Q3 or Q6; but the evidence of the readings
has been thought to be so conflicting between the two as to
lead only to a sterile controversy that has tended to bring
textual discussion as a whole into some disrepute. In 1885
P. A. Daniel found 8 readings peculiar to Q6 and the Folio,
to which he added 3 instances (only 2 of which were legitimate) of conjectural emendation in the Folio of errors
peculiar to Q6. In 1955 J. K. Walton put forward Q3 as the
sole candidate. Analysis of his arguments shows that he can
offer only 2 true cases of verbal readings uniquely shared by
Q3 and the Folio,[1] although he conceals this disheartening
shortage by sandwiching them in a longer list of 22 'readings
peculiar to Q3 and F—peculiar to Q3 and F, that is, when
we ignore quartos coming after Q3'. Since all but these two
are shared by Q6 as well, the 20 superfluous readings
common to Q3 and Q6 scarcely serve as evidence to govern
a decision between the two quartos.

One can place 2 readings pointing to Q3 against 11 or 12
favouring Q6. This is precious little evidence on which to
decide the case, and one's confidence is not increased by the
minor nature of some of the shared Q6 and F verbals. Two
concern the use of a natural singular instead of an equally
natural plural, a variation the compositors frequently fell
into from memorial error. Common idiom or the possibility
of independent memorial contamination from the context

---

[1] These are Q3–4, F agreement in *no manner person* versus Q1–2, *5–6 manner of
person* (III. v. 108), and Q3, F *I bury* [Q3 *burie*] versus Q1–2 *I buried* and Q4–6
Ile burie. A third concurrence is not noted: this is Q3, F *it is* versus Q1–2, 4–6 *is it*
(IV. ii. 82). However, since *it is* appears to be correct, one could argue for Q6 copy *is
it* altered by the annotator to *it is*, and the effect of the Q3, F concurrence vanishes.

cast some doubt on a few others, so that if one disregards the cumulative weight of insignificant agreements, no more than three or four readings remain common to Q6 and F that on any individual basis might perhaps offer valid evidence.

That in truth this cumulative evidence can be ignored is Mr. Walton's proposition. Independent analysis confirms in some part the principle behind his position (although not necessarily his application). Actually, it is only the unique readings shared by the Folio with one or other quarto that can have any textual significance. This uniqueness need not be narrowly interpreted, however, in any absolute sense: once all quartos except Q3 and Q6 have been eliminated, any reading is unique for the purposes of decision between Q3 and Q6 (no matter how shared with other quartos) so long as it is not shared by the two surviving competitors. Yet despite the most liberal interpretation placed on the question of uniqueness, it is inevitable that any terminal edition is likely to agree uniquely with its chronological predecessors more often than with an earlier edition, even though the earlier edition is the copy-text and the immediate predecessor is not.[1]

Any reading that is not so obviously wrong or eccentric or in need of modernization as to be independently corrected will in normal course be passed on from the edition in which it originates to all descendants in the same line.[2] The Third Quarto of *Richard III* has about 42 substantive readings diverging from Q1–2 that are accepted by the Folio. However, 39 of these 42 were passed on through Q4–5 to Q6 as well. Thus the only verbal readings that can be used as evidence in favour of Q3 are Q3 variants from Q1–2 that in turn were varied further by Q6 but appear in the Folio in

---

[1] Of course, the 'predecessor' must derive genetically from the 'early edition' in question so that it shares readings with this early edition.

[2] That is, the fortuitous agreement in unique readings between a terminal edition and its immediate chronological predecessor (though not its copy-text) will ordinarily outnumber the unique agreements with an early edition that was the copy-text, provided the conditions stated above in footnote 1 are met.

their Q3 form. These conditions are so stringent as to remove almost all possibility that agreement of substantive
readings alone could ever prove that Q3 served as copy for
the Folio.

Correspondingly, evidence that is not necessarily significant, although it may seem so, will usually accumulate in
the chronological predecessor of a terminal edition even
though one does not derive from the other. In this text 1
reading that originated in Q4 and 2 in Q5 may be added to
the 12 originating in Q6 to make a total of 15 that are
uniquely shared by Q6 and the Folio against Q3. Mr.
Walton has very properly pointed out the odds that these
are fortuitous. For example, if we make a comparison we
find that 17 unique readings are shared by the 1623 Folio
with Q7 of 1629, and 9 different unique readings with Q8 of
1634, both quartos that could not possibly have served as
copy-text for F. Moreover, there is no credible evidence that
F in any way influenced these two quartos. Not all of these
readings are of equal strength, but there are enough that are
pertinent to give one pause. Mr. Walton takes these statistics
as automatically disproving the significance of the set of 12
(actually 15) that Q6 shares uniquely with F. Of course,
they do nothing of the kind, for the Q6 readings could still
be legitimate evidence; and Mr. Walton gives us no idea of
what we should expect in the way of agreement if Q6 had
indeed been the copy.

However, the evidence from Q7 and Q8 does have its
value in enforcing caution before the Q6 list is accepted as
valid. With only a few exceptions these readings from Q6
may be fortuitous, or they may be significant. The point is,
we do not know. Hence the dispute about *Richard III* shows
the inadequacy of conventional methods to solve the problem
of Folio copy-text when an annotated quarto is a possibility.
Because in *Richard III* the transmission of the text through
a series of prints allows identifiable corruption to be transmitted to the Folio, the difficulty is not present (as it is with

Hamlet and *2 Henry IV*) in deciding whether the F copy-text was a manuscript or annotated printed copy. But the almost insuperable problem remains of determining which of the two ultimate quarto candidates was the actual copy-text. The unique readings originating in any intermediate quarto like Q3 are almost all passed on to its successors so that the odds are almost prohibitive against more than one or two remaining unique between it and the Folio to act as evidence.

Correspondingly, the usual forces of correction and corruption will inevitably produce a group of shared readings between any terminal edition and the one chronologically just before it, as may be seen in the coincidences between *Richard III* F and Q7. Examples of this process may make us wary of accepting readings as significant evidence when they are not so incontrovertible in their nature or so extraordinary in their profusion as to enforce belief. Most of the readings shared in *Richard III* by the Folio and Q6 do not qualify under these rigorous requirements, although several are not easy to explain away. Nor, it may be said, do the readings of Q3 qualify either.

Yet it is difficult to know how a critic is to judge what is an acceptable quantity or quality of evidence. Something will depend upon his estimate of the annotator's care. For instance, if Q3 were the copy-text for F *Richard III*, the corrector discarded 97 of its original divergences from Q2 and returned these to the Q1 readings, which were presumably those of the manuscript. If Q6 had been the copy-text, the corrector would have returned 110 of its original divergences to the Q1 forms. These figures are so close as to be useless. If we properly add to the 97 Q3 variants the 46 Q2 divergences from Q1 accepted by Q3 but returned by F to the Q1 forms, we have a total of 143 readings in which Q3 differed from Q1, and F agreed with Q1. But it seems meaningless to discover that by the time the accumulated textual corruption was passed on to Q6, the corrector would have rejected a total of 287 Q6 readings in favour of the Q1 verbals. Whether more of this large number should have slipped through into the Folio in their Q6 form than the noticed 15 is a matter of opinion that is not demonstrable one way or the other.

Mr. Walton takes it as significant that some 22 (actually about 42) readings that in Q3 differed from Q1 (though shared by Q6) were accepted by the Folio, versus only 12 (actually 15) originating in Q6. But by this line of argument Q2 would qualify for serious consideration, since of its 74 divergences from Q1 the Folio corrector would have passed 28 while rejecting 46 if it had been the copy. That the annotator—if Q6 had been the copy—would have rejected 110 of the variants originating in Q6 while accepting only 15 seems at first sight disproportionate, especially in view of the small number of divergences in Q4 and Q5 that proved acceptable. Nevertheless, it would seem that in this text the big push to 'correctness', or normality, was made in Q2 and Q3, and after this stage the additional variants, especially those in Q6, were evident corruptions of a nature to call themselves most obviously to the annotator's attention.

III. *Compositorial Spellings as Bibliographical Evidence*

Whatever line of inquiry we take, we are forced back to the original position that in either of the two categories of annotated quartos the traditional evidence of substantive readings has not solved, and often cannot solve, the special problems involved in the positive identification of copy-text with enough force to receive general acceptance. And if this is so, the verbal readings are even more useless to settle difficult questions that have been raised whether pages from one or from more than one edition were brought together to form the printer's copy.

Under these circumstances it is proper to inquire whether bibliographical methods cannot be applied to the general problem in the hope of securing evidence that will be supplementary and perhaps even decisive. The two major problems

that have been solved by the demonstration of printed copy—
King Lear and *Troilus and Cressida*—each succumbed to
different kinds of bibliographical evidence; in the one instance the forms of press-corrections, and in the other the
forms of speech-prefixes and the variable use of italic in the
setting of names. Neither of these methods is very useful
in the other plays, and hence—pending the discovery of
some other technique—it would seem that the remaining
problems must be attacked by a study of the transmission of
the accidental readings, that is, the details of spelling,
capitalization, punctuation, and word-division in which the
substantives are clothed. These will be combined, of course,
with whatever other evidence from the mechanical printing
process that suggests itself as significant.

In preparing annotated quartos, the annotator's concern
to bring the wording of the print into conformity with the
manuscript wipes out most of the evidence one customarily
secures from the transmission of substantive variants in
normal reprints. We may not suppose that in all instances the
corrector was indifferent to the accidentals of the printed
copy, and in fact it can be shown that in some categories he
might indeed alter them to accord with the manuscript form.
But many—if not the majority—of the divergences in the
accidentals in control reprint texts appear to have been un-
touched, and it is from these that the hoped-for evidence
must derive, since they alone can be inferred to have escaped
the corrective process.

The use of spelling tests to separate and to identify compositors is now well established, and a handful of studies have
appeared separating the work of various compositors in
Elizabethan play quartos. These spelling tests identify compositors by the positive evidence of their habitual or characteristic trend towards imposing their own spellings on the
copy being set. That is, the evidence consists exclusively of
the compositors' divergences from copy. On the contrary,
the technique of establishing the nature of the copy from

which a compositor set rests on examples of the compositor's agreement with his copy; that is, on the evidence of the occasions in which his copy influenced the compositor either to forsake his habitual characteristics or else to choose the copy form a remarkable number of times when his own practice was largely indifferent.

Irregularity in the copy being tested is usually a desideratum. For instance, if the assumed copy agrees with the compositor's known spelling habits for a word, nothing is proved when he sets the word according to his habitual spelling. Moreover, unless irregularity is present, the concurrence of spelling in indifferent forms cannot be detected. As an example, a text might spell *feel* consistently as *feele*, but if a compositor used this edition and set a number of *feel* forms, as well as *feele*, the concurrences in *feele* would be meaningless as evidence for derivation whenever the compositor's practice was ordinarily indifferent and therefore without detectable preference.

Most attempts to establish the influence of one or other form of copy on a given edition have been unsystematic and partial. Both faults have been forced on the undertakers by the difficulty that no complete spelling and other accidentals analysis exists for any Elizabethan compositor other than a few of the most conspicuous ways in which he diverged from copy. This situation has been brought about, of course, by the inquiry into compositorial spellings chiefly from the point of view of departures from copy, evidence from which compositors could be identified and separated. Words in which these compositors were likely to be influenced by copy have been so valueless for the purpose of identification (except as a contrast to a marked characteristic of another compositor being compared) as to escape notice.

Thus those critics who have tried to use the evidence of the accidentals have had a tendency to ignore the compositor altogether and have unsystematically chosen various examples of what they regarded as copy eccentricities repeated in the

Folio text, arguing for these as evidence of the direct connexion of the two texts. No proof is usually advanced that
these were indeed eccentricities in the original, and that the
corresponding form in the Folio text was not possible or
customary for the compositor to use, or could not have
derived ultimately from a common original. Hence because
this is partial and subjective selection of evidence without a
basis in ascertained fact, no case has been or could have been
advanced that has touched the borders of proof; and the
abuse of the method has served only to arouse scepticism
about the validity of accidentals as evidence.

The other method, of attempting to explain divergences
from habitual spellings as due to the influence of copy, is
more easily approached because of some information that has
accumulated about Compositors A and B in the Folio. But,
again, this information has concentrated on discovering their
mutually opposed habitual spellings rather than those in
which they were subject to the influence of copy. And in
addition test words and the degree of fidelity to be expected
with them are not wholly trustworthy, because the evidence
for B was compiled before he was distinguished from E, and
the evidence for A does not as yet distinguish him from C,
who has been partly included in pre-Hinman analyses.

Pending a more satisfactory statistical study of A and of B,
it has seemed possible to illustrate and in some sort to test the
technique for the investigation of mechanical evidence by
a provisional study of Compositor E, the workman whom
Dr. Hinman has identified as an apprentice.[1] This workman
set from printed copy almost all of the Folio *Titus Andronicus*, and *Romeo and Juliet*. He also set the first 3 pages of the
original *Troilus and Cressida*, $13\frac{1}{2}$ pages of the Folio *King
Lear*, 6 of *Othello*, and 4 of *Hamlet*.

Several factors favour such a study. First, an inexperienced

---

[1] 'The Prentice Hand in the Tragedies of the Shakespeare First Folio', *Studies
in Bibliography*, ix (1957), 3–20.

and therefore cautious compositor might be supposed to feel
the influence of copy more strongly than a thoroughly
routined workman, and it should be of some interest to see
if this deduction is valid as applied to E. Second, E set two
plays, and three pages of another, from printed copy that as
a whole had not been corrected, and these should provide
adequate information about the influence of copy on his
setting of accidentals. To these may be added a third in-
centive. Compositor E set some pages in *King Lear*, *Othello*,
and *Hamlet*, all plays that in one textual respect or another are
in dispute; and it may be that fresh evidence can assist in our
taking a firmer view about the nature of their copy-texts.
Finally the total amount of Folio text set by E is not so large
that an attempt may not be made to study his work in relation to copy without an electronic computer or old-spelling
concordance.[1] Undoubtedly, some of his indifferent characteristics that cumulatively would be of the highest value to
know will not be apparent without mechanical computation.
Nevertheless, even though the hoped-for results may be only
provisional, if they are at all positive they should be of interest as an exercise in method, and they may produce some useful hints towards the solution of a problem or two.

iv. *Compositor E and the Folio* Othello

Compositor E was first identified by Dr. Hinman on
evidence that was completely mechanical. While A and B
were setting *Coriolanus*, *Julius Caesar*, and *Macbeth*, one or
other of their type-cases was being used at the same time
by someone else to set intercalary formes of *Titus* and of
Romeo, plays before and after the texts with which A and B
were concerned. Dr. Hinman ingeniously suggested that

---

[1] The emphasis here is on *study*. No definitive account of E and his relation to
copy can be made without laborious hand-indexing of every word he set, or the
computer sorting of the same evidence from the text on tapes. What follows, therefore, is at best a trial investigation from selected, not from bulk, evidence. Evidence
from the texts of *Hamlet* and *King Lear* has been excluded since the copy-text for the
Folio is still in some measure in dispute, and only the parts of *Titus*, *Romeo*, and
Troilus have been used as controls.

this stranger E was an apprentice who was trusted only with printed copy and who worked, at first, while A and B were setting from manuscripts. Compositor E would take over the type-cases from either one when he was absent from the Folio and presumably busy about some other job in the shop involving a different fount of type. This new workman began setting with *Titus Andronicus* (from Q3 of 1611) and followed with *Romeo and Juliet* (from Q3 of 1609). The sheets were more carefully proof-corrected than were those set by the other Folio compositors, and indeed the need for such a review is shown by the considerable number of mechanical errors, such as mis-spacings and transpositions and also loosened types indicating improper justification. After completing *Romeo and Juliet* he started *Troilus and Cressida* from an unannotated copy of the quarto. But when work on this was halted after three pages, he may be said to have graduated. When A departed from the Folio towards the end of *Macbeth*, and C also, towards the end of *Hamlet*, E worked in regular conjunction with B through the last pages of *Hamlet* and all through *King Lear*; and he set the first six pages of *Othello* (i. i. 1 to i. iii. 391), starting in the same formes as his last two pages of *Lear* in gathering ss, until B came in to set the outer forme of the outermost sheet of ss. Thereafter B took over and set the remainder of the Folio unaided until A returned at the very end to speed *Troilus and Cressida* and complete the volume.

Compositor E was very likely John Leason, son of John Leason of Husley in Hampshire. He was bound to William Jaggard on 4 November 1622,[1] a few months before Dr. Hinman estimates work was started on *Titus*. The identification seems plausible since it is indeed clear that E was not an expert typesetter, and the apprentice bound immediately before Leason was Laurence Yardsley as far back as 1614. The date at which Leason was made free is not recorded.

[1] D. F. McKenzie, 'A List of Printers' Apprentices, 1605–1640', *Studies in Bibliography*, xiii (1960), 125.

Compositor E was not allowed to set the first page of *Titus* or of *Romeo*, presumably because the balance and spacing of the head-title and ornament might have caused him trouble. He did set the first page of the original *Troilus and Cressida*, but not of *King Lear*, and he was allowed to start with the first page of *Othello*. It may be that some mislineation at the beginning of *Othello* was caused by the trouble he experienced in adjusting text about the ornamental initial letter that headed I. i.

Dr. Alice Walker's argument for the use of the Quarto as copy-text for the Folio *Othello* catches at several pieces of evidence that are susceptible of other explanation and finally comes to rest on a combination of orthographical similarity and common error. Given the verbal divergences in the two texts that demonstrate a tendency to verbal substitution in the Quarto, 'it is very remarkable to find that [Q] agrees with the Folio in readings such as "This present warres", "Toth' very moment" (I. iii. 133), "morties", "lushious", "my currant runnes", and so on. It is, in fact, only possible to reconcile the evidence of the verbal variants between the printed texts with their close orthographical connexion, common errors, and common typographical features by supposing that the Folio text was printed (with correction and amplification) from a copy of the Quarto.'[1]

Since the orthographical evidence adduced is confined to a handful of examples without reference to established compositorial characteristics,[2] I propose to bring to bear on the problem some spelling evidence gathered from a study of Compositor E's habits, and therefore confined to the first six pages of the Folio text (I. i. 1 to I. iii. 391), to suggest that Dr. Walker is indeed correct in her general assumption. My purpose here is not to demonstrate the nature of the copy beyond all question—a task too lengthy and complex for oral

---

[1] 'The 1622 Quarto and the First Folio Texts of *Othello*', *Shakespeare Survey*, 5 (1952), 23.

[2] See note E, pp. 199–201.

presentation[1]—but to illustrate some of the possibilities of a different method of investigation from the conventional use of verbals or of undifferentiated spelling 'hits'.

As with Compositors A and B in the Folio, the three best words with which to test Compositor E are *do*, *go*, and *here*. Fortunately, he was much more willing to accept copy spellings of these than were A and B, and though he had a preference for the short forms *do* and *go*, and the long form *heere*, we find in the control texts that he set numerous examples of *doe*, *goe*, and *here* when the copy encouraged them. However, he would very seldom indeed set one of his non-preferential forms against a copy that had his favourite spelling, and then ordinarily in prose when he was perhaps justifying his line.

That E could be influenced by his copy is well illustrated by his treatment of the word *here*. The characteristics of the *Titus* and *Romeo* quartos vary widely in respect to this word. The *Titus* Q3 compositor set a vast majority of the long form *heere*, whereas the *Romeo* Q3 compositor set a vast majority of the short forme *here*. In each play E's characteristics are correspondingly affected. In *Titus* Q3 appear 65 *heere* spellings that E followed,[2] 11 *here* forms changed to *heere* by E, 1 anomalous *heere* changed to *here*, and 3 *here* spellings reproduced in the Folio. But in the Folio *Romeo* 60 short forms are repeated from Q3 and only 9 short forms are changed to long. In *Troilus* 3 *heere* spellings are followed, 4 *here* forms are changed to *heere*, 1 *heere* to *here* (an anomaly in a prose passage), and 3 short *here* spellings are reproduced.

The pattern in E's six pages of *Othello* follows that in *Romeo* where the conditions were roughly the same, and is not inconsistent with the evidence of *Troilus*. Of 15 occurrences in *Othello* the Folio follows the unusual long form twice,

---

[1] A more detailed study of Compositor E is in preparation.

[2] Although the statistics in this chapter have been independently checked, data of this sort secured by inspection and not by computer may vary slightly in absolute accuracy.

changes *here* to *heere* 3 times, and reproduces Q's short *here* 10 times. By itself the treatment of this word does not show that the Quarto was the copy for the Folio, but it strongly indicates that, whatever the printer's copy, it must have corresponded very closely to the characteristics of the Quarto in respect to the spelling of this word. On E's record in the control texts, the Folio copy must have had a majority spelling of *here*. That the copy's preferential form might have been *heere* is a hypothesis that cannot be entertained.

From *Titus* through *Romeo* and on to *Troilus* we see Compositor E hardening in his preference for the short form of *do*. In *Titus* 25 short *do* forms are followed, 22 *doe* spellings are shortened to *do*, but 39 long *doe* spellings are reproduced. In *Romeo* 44 short Q forms are followed, 19 long forms are changed to short, and only 13 long forms are followed, with one anomalous change of short to long, in verse. In *Troilus* 10 short forms are followed, and the only 3 long forms are shortened. There is one anomalous change of short to long, but in a prose passage.

The statistics for *Othello* do not suggest that the printer's copy was very mixed in its characteristics but instead that it ran strongly to the long *doe* form. In the Quarto 34 of the 35 examples are spelled *doe*, which the Folio sets as *do* in 30 cases, agreeing with Q *doe* in 4 occurrences and with Q *do* in its single appearance. The figure of 4 repeats is about what we should expect to slip through Compositor E at this stage of his experience when setting from copy that ran strongly against his preferential short form. Thus whatever the copy-text was for Folio *Othello* it would seem to have resembled the Quarto fairly closely in its spelling of this word.

Compositor E's treatment of *go* is not so rigorous as what he does with *do*. In *Titus* the invariable Q *goe* is changed to *go* only 6 times and is followed on 32 occasions. In *Romeo* 16 long forms are followed, 3 long forms are shortened, and 51 short forms are reproduced. In the three pages of *Troilus*, E follows *go* twice, *goe* twice, and alters one *goe* to *go*.

By the time *Othello* was set, E was opting more firmly for the short form, with the result that of the 12 occurrences of the word in his stint he set 10 as *go* and only 2 as *goe*. In this group the 2 short Q spellings are short in F, but 8 of the *goe* spellings appear as *go* in F and in only 2 of the Q *goe* forms is there agreement.

At the least, one can say that, in view of the evidence, if Folio *Othello* were set from a manuscript, the manuscript must have been very close indeed to the Quarto practice in the mixed charateristics of these three words, with a predominance—as in the Quarto—of the forms *here*, *doe*, and *goe*.

But the evidence can be viewed more narrowly. Not much, if any, significance attaches to the fact that the one time Q *Othello* set *do* and the two times it set *go*, the Folio agrees, although if a manuscript had been the copy, and the long forms were in these places, chance might have led E to follow the non-preferential spelling. But with *here* we have a different situation. There are only 5 *heere* spellings in the Folio *Othello* set by E as against 10 *here* forms, and it would seem to be more significant that the only 2 times that the Quarto printed the long form *heere*, it also appears in the Folio. That is, 2 of the 5 preferential *heere* spellings in the Folio would have come from the Quarto. The 2-to-1 setting of *here* in F does not produce a *here* in the only two places where Q spelled *heere*.

This agreement is not beyond chance, of course, but if we combine the odds against this happening for *here* with the added odds for the *goe* agreement twice out of the 10 long forms in the Quarto, we may find it logically significant that in no case in these three words in *Othello* (and Q is mixed in its characteristics for all three) does a non-preferential E spelling in the Folio appear when there was a preferential spelling in the Quarto. This result corresponds to the evidence from the control texts that never more than once in any single text does E set a non-preferential form against a preferential. Whether this unusual result in *Othello* might have been achieved if the Folio had been set from an independent manuscript, the characteristics of which must certainly have differed in some respects from the Quarto print, may remain a matter of opinion. But, at least, the evidence should persuade us to entertain a working hypothesis that the Quarto was the copy-text for the Folio, since there is nothing in the evidence contrary to that hypothesis and some positive indications that favour it.

Yet if we continue to test the possibility that a manuscript was the copy, nevertheless, we find that this hypothetical copy and the Quarto would seem to have agreed in another respect, in spelling *answer* at least a few times without a final -*e*. In *Titus* the 3 times the word appears it is spelled *answere* in Q and F (*aunswere* in Q at ii. iii. 298), and in *Romeo and Juliet* both texts agree 8 times in *answere* although once F changes Q *answere* to *answer* and once the unique Q *answer* to *answere*. In *Troilus* E follows copy twice in *answere* and once in repeating *answer*. In the 5 times the word appears in *Othello*, the Q spelling is invariably *answer*, which F follows twice while altering the remaining 3 times to *answere*. The short form, uncharacteristic of E, would seem to have been produced by his following copy.

Ordinarily Compositor E follows copy in setting *heauen* with a lower-case *h* or a capital *H*, although he has a general tendency to capitalize when a change is made. Never in *Titus* and *Romeo* does he reduce a capital *Heauen* to lower-case. This being so, the evidence in Folio *Othello* is of considerable interest. Of the 7 occurrences of the word, 1 comes in an added Folio passage (set from manuscript) where it is capitalized. Folio and Quarto agree once in the capital, and twice the Folio raises Q lower-case to capitals. Interestingly, the only 3 times that *heauen* appears in E's stint in F *Othello*, it reproduces Q's use of lower-case. Whether or not it is chance that the single Q capitalization is also capitalized in F, the fact is apparent—given E's characteristics—that the F copy-text must have read *heauen* a majority of the times (Q is 5 to 1 for *heauen*), else the 3 lower-case spellings would not have appeared in F. (In *Titus* 19 cases of *heauen*, which is invariable, are reproduced in F; in *Romeo* 26 lower-case are followed, 1 capital is followed, and 1 lower-case is raised to a capital.)

A sprinkling of other spelling or accidentals evidence is not worth mentioning at present because of a lack of full information, such as the QF agreement in *inioynted* whereas E ordinarily alters such prefixes to *en-*. However, E normally seems to follow copy in *honor–honour* although he may have some slight preference for the *-our* form. For instance, in *Titus* he follows *honour* 10 times, *honor* once, and alters one *honor* to *honour*; in *Romeo* he follows *honour* 4 times, and raises the single *honor* to *honour*. There may be significance, then, to the *Othello* QF agreement in the only two appearances of the singular, once as *honor* and once as *honour*, although plural *honors* is altered in F to *honours* in its one occurrence. Such words can be multiplied, but they are too scattered and unsystematic according to our present information to offer convincing evidence in themselves.

Typographical evidence is not very weighty, although it is consistent with the emerging picture of F as derived from Q. For instance, in *Othello* E rejects the Q italicizing of names of countries and of nationalities, such as *Cyprus* and *Turk*. It may be, therefore, that the F italics in *Ottamites* and *Ottoman* that correspond to Q's and go contrary to E's usual practice resulted from E's unfamiliarity with the words, just as he followed Q in italicizing *Anthropophagie* although reducing Q's italics in *Canibals* to roman. The splitting of pentameter lines in F that may follow Q is of no significance: E very seldom turns under or over a long line and almost invariably prefers to set such as two independent lines, breaking at the caesura. Thus a line so long that Q would break it would automatically be broken by E regardless of its form in his copy.

Some minor information of this sort bearing on the

accidentals[1] can be skipped in favour of three concluding pieces of evidence.

The common readings like *lushious* and the name *Luccicos*, noticed by Dr. Walker, could come from a common source as she recognizes. But the false emendation of an error is customarily taken as excellent proof of direct genetic relationship, and thus—while far from conclusive in itself—may be utilized, in view of the accumulation of evidence retailed above, as a strong corroboration once a working hypothesis has been established from spelling evidence in favour of the Quarto having served as copy-text for the Folio. At i. iii. 230, as Dr. Walker points out, Othello's phrase *the flinty and steel couch of war* is misprinted in Q as *Cooch* and in F is falsely corrected to *Coach*. This is so little the sort of error one could assign to a common original that the conclusion seems natural that the Q error was overlooked by the annotator and badly rationalized by E, or (perhaps more probable) that E misread the annotator's correction of *u* as *a*. In either case, the Quarto must have been the physical printer's copy.

The remaining two are much more speculative, and they could hardly be mentioned at all as evidence except after the establishment of a working hypothesis. Neither has been noticed previously.

Othello i. iii. 106 in the Quarto reads

Du. To youth this is no proofe,

whereas the Folio omits the speech-prefix in error and alters to read

To vouch this, is no proofe,

It is tempting to speculate that the annotator in correcting the error *youth* to *vouch* in some manner seemed to E to have deleted the speech-prefix. The fact that the prefix is wrongly

---

[1] As, for instance, the treatment of round brackets. In *Titus* and *Romeo* E adds 6 pairs of round brackets while dropping only 1. In his short stint in *Troilus* he increases this tendency by adding 3, as many as in the whole of either full control play. In *Othello* he freely adds 31, retains the 2 present in the Q, and drops none. Chance might dictate, thus, that F could agree with the two Q pairs, regardless of the nature of the copy, but the evidence, still, is not inconsistent with the view that F was set from Q.

omitted at the very point where the start of the line is emended in the Folio could well be significant.

When the conflicting reports about the Turkish fleet are being brought to the Venetian council, a messenger arrives. In the Quarto at I. iii. 12 his speech-prefix is *One within*, and a line of text is followed by the stage-direction *Enter a Messenger*, who thereupon has two speeches, each headed by the prefix *Sailor* spelled with an *i*. In the Folio the corresponding forms are *Saylor within* and *Enter Saylor*, with a *y*. However, the first Folio prefix is *Officer* (substituting for Q *Sailor*) and then, for the first time (line 14) F sets the prefix *Sailor* but with an anomalous *i*. Given the two settings of *Saylor* with *y* in a passage of written alteration when the Quarto read respectively *One* and *Messenger*, the conjecture is attractive that the speech-prefix with an *i* at line 14 resulted from E following the Quarto's form *Sailor* the one time he would have been setting this word from print. In the circumstances it is unfortunate that the word does not occur in any of the control texts set by E and thus no proof is available whether *saylor* or *sailor* was his preferential form, or whether he was inclined to follow copy without preference.

It would seem, then, that Dr. Walker was admirably right to challenge received opinion and to assert that the Folio *Othello* was set from an amplified and altered copy of the print of Q1. The application attempted here of a provisional and certainly incomplete analysis of Compositor E[1] has, I hope, confirmed the somewhat sketchy evidence heretofore available by the introduction of another range of evidence based on ascertained compositorial characteristics[2] of the

---

[1] The full case must, of course, await an analysis of Compositor B in relation to the Quarto. At the present moment, however, although we have some information about B's divergences from copy of the sort that usefully distinguishes him from Compositor A, we do not have a full-scale study of how he followed copy. D. F. McKenzie's 'Compositor B's Role in *The Merchant of Venice*, Q2 (1619)', *Studies in Bibliography*, xii (1959), 75–89, makes an excellent start on the problem.

[2] The emphasis here is on *ascertained* evidence about an identified compositor drawn from control texts and applied to the problem at hand.

kind that would most likely escape the hand of the annotator.[1]

Indeed, it appears in all problems of these annotated play
quartos that substantive readings alone have failed to settle
vexed questions of copy-text in any manner that has secured
general approval of the results on evidence that appears to
demonstrate the case. The hand of the annotator has so
frequently destroyed or concealed evidence from the verbals
of the text that significant coincidences generally available
in simple reprints dwindle in marked-up copy into incon-
clusive similarities. Most substantive errors that can be
trusted to be errors are ordinarily subject to the counter-
hypothesis of independent transmission from a common
original.[2] Thus the only evidence in ordinary circumstances
that is not susceptible to significant change by this annotation and that is copious enough to be of use in tackling
difficult problems of mixed copy is the evidence from the
transmission of the accidentals.

Nevertheless, it is idle to attempt to apply concurrences in
these accidentals except on the basis of a thoroughgoing
compositorial analysis. Concurrence can be meaningless if
the Folio and Quarto compositors' characteristics or usual
spellings are the same. That the Folio *Othello* follows the
Quarto in the divided *my selfe* but the run-together *himselfe*
is of no consequence when one knows that the identical distinction is habitual with Compositor E. That the Folio
religiously agrees with the Quarto in the full form of all
-lesse and *-nesse* endings is meaningless when we know that by

---

[1] An annotator can, it is clear, occasionally concern himself with relatively
common words, as evidenced by *Othello* Q *darlings* but F *Deareling* at I. ii. 68, a
change not otherwise observed in E's work. If *2 Henry IV* were indeed set from annotated printed copy, the extensive alteration of remarkably small points would constitute a very special case.

[2] Moreover, such evidence is not frequent enough to settle difficult questions of
mixed copy such as has been asserted exists in F *King Lear* by A. S. Cairncross, 'The
Quarto and the Folio Text of *King Lear*', *Review of English Studies*, N.S., vi (1955),
252–8.

the time he came to *Othello* Compositor E never set anything else, regardless of his copy. Concurrence can also be meaningless if the spelling agreement derives from the habitual practice of the Folio workman regardless of the mixed habits of the Quarto compositor. Thus any attempt to argue for Quarto copy in a Folio text set by Compositor B is doomed to failure if the Quarto has irregularly set *do* or *doe*, and the 'hits' in the short form are taken as significant. Compositor B was so confirmed in his preference for the spelling *do* that his regularity (or his rare lapses) give us no hint in this respect about the nature of the underlying copy from which he was setting.

Random 'hits' that cannot be confirmed as significant are highly misleading used as evidence. Possibly F *Off-capt* and Q *Oft capt* (1. i. 10) constitute evidence in their agreement in the *-t* ending, but no means exist to demonstrate the conjecture when this is the only use of the preterite in Shakespeare, according to the Concordance. Moreover, analogy often does not work in establishing spelling characteristics. For instance, one compositor of Q2 *Romeo and Juliet* is an inveterate *-ie* speller but he consistently spells *Lady* and *body*.[1] Thus it is not enough in any case to argue from the assumed evidence of similar words: the exact words, and only these exact words, can constitute evidence, or else such forms as influence spelling without regard for the word itself. It may be (I do not know) that this compositor in Q2 *Romeo and Juliet* would set all words with *-ie* endings except for the combination *-dy*. Certainly such inexplicable distinctions may be observed in many Elizabethan compositors. In *Othello* Compositor E set at least 19 words in *-ly* and only 3 in *-lie*, but

[1] George Walton Williams, 'The Printing of *Romeo and Juliet* (1599)', *Studies in Bibliography*, ix (1957), 111. Dr. Williams privately informs me that *lady* appears at least 34 times and *ladie* not at all save for *Ladie-bird* reproducing Q1 *Ladie bird* in a reprinted passage. *Body* occurs 7 times and *bodie* not at all. For *ready* and *already* the compositor is indifferent: *ready* appears 3 times and *readie* twice; *already* twice and *alreadie* once. For all other nouns and adjectives he is a *-die* speller, as in *bandie* (1), *bloudie* (5), *studie* (1), *unwieldie* (1), and *tardie* (1).

21 in *-tie* versus 7 in *-ty*. Obviously, until one analyses the preceding consonant(s) nothing can be said about any habits he may have had in ending words with *-ie* or *-y*, and any attempt at a statistical study of the undifferentiated evidence would offer a most misleading picture.[1]

What seem to be somewhat odd individual spellings that agree in two texts may turn out not to be so odd after all, or else susceptible of explanation as deriving from a common source. An eager critic might, just for example, seize on *Gardiners* in both Q and F *Othello* (I. iii. 324), only to find that *Hamlet* Q2 *Gardners* (v. i. 34) is changed by E (if Q2 were the copy-text) to Folio *Gardiners*. Whether *Epithites* in QF *Othello* is a significant agreement is not to be determined, since *epithet* is not found elsewhere in E's work. Whether Q *syen* and F *Seyen* (I. iii. 337) for *scion* is evidence for Q copy-text or for common derivation from an eccentric manuscript spelling is surely not demonstrable in the lack of evidence from controls.

Just as insufficient to bear the weight of any hypothesis is the quotation of passages of generally similar accidentals. We may compare a random passage from *King Lear* to see what this sort of impressionistic or merely statistical evidence could reveal about the problem of Q1 or Q2 copy. Here is I. i. 248–60 in the Folio, with all accidentals italicized that differ between Q1 and Q2 where F agrees with one or the other:

> *Bur.* I am *sorry* then you haue so lost a Father,
> That you must *loose* a husband.
>   *Cor.* Peace be with *Burgundie,*
> Since that respect and Fortunes are his loue,
> I shall not be his wife.
>   *Fra.* Fairest *Cordelia,* that art most rich being poore,
> Most choise forsaken, and most lou'd *despis'd,*
> Thee and thy vertues *here* I *seize* vpon,
> Be it lawful I take vp *what's* cast *away.*

[1] See note F, p. 201.

Gods, Gods! 'Tis strange, that from their *cold'st* neglect
My Loue should kindle to enflam'd respect.
Thy *dowrelesse* Daughter *King*, throwne to my chance,
Is Queene of vs, of ours, and our faire France:

The respective readings are:

F	Q1	Q2
sorry	sory	*sorry*
loose	*loose*	lose
Burgundie	*Burgundie*	Burgundy
Cordelia,	~ ‸	*Cordelia,*
despis'd	despisd	*despis'd*
here	*here*	heere
seize	ceaze	*seize*
what's	whats	*what's*
away.	~,	*away.*
cold'st	couldst	*cold'st*
enflam'd	inflam'd	*enflam'd*
dowrelesse	dowreles	*dowrelesse*
King,	~ ‸	*King,*

Of 13 differences in the accidentals, F agrees with Q2 10 times and with Q1 only 3 times. Yet this raw statistical concurrence cannot take account of the number of times that the agreement of Q2 and F can have no significance since E's customary practice is being reflected in F, not necessarily the influence of Q2 copy. With these cases out of the way, the evidence becomes almost wholly neutral except for the powerful effect of the concurrence of F and Q1 in Compositor E's non-preferential *here* versus Q2's *heere*. After all that we know of E's treatment of this word in the control texts, to suppose that E has gone against Q2 copy and set non-preferential *here* in this passage is infinitely more difficult than to explain away the largely insignificant agreements of F with Q2. Thus unanalysed statistical evidence must always be viewed with reserve. It may mean much, or nothing.

Wanting such strict bibliographical evidence as can be

drawn most happily from the typographical irregularities of *Troilus and Cressida*, the only other trustworthy method (when substantive evidence fails) is to assemble some quantity of examples in which the Folio compositor broke with his own ascertained preferential habits in order to follow the Quarto spellings or significantly agreed with these when his own practice was largely indifferent. Individually most of these small pieces of evidence may seem to be of little consequence; yet when they have been properly analysed from control texts and when they point in the same direction, their cumulative agreement exerts a powerful leverage. But obviously this evidence cannot qualify for serious consideration unless one knows one's compositor and has some information about the amount of variation that can be expected under specified control conditions that approximate those under examination.

Finally, when the case is not just one of deciding which of two printed editions was the copy-text (as in the *Richard III* problem) but instead is one of deciding between a lost manuscript and an annotated copy of a known quarto (as in *Othello*), a further leverage can be exerted by another form of evidence, one that may be described as qualitative.

Quantitative evidence may be defined as the normal estimated percentage that an identified compositor will set a non-preferential form when his copy-text is invariable or nearly invariable in printing the non-preferential spelling. For instance, in Q *Othello* appear 34 spellings *doe* and 1 *do*. The argument in favour of Q copy-text for F concerns E's strong attachment to the short *do* spelling that leads him to alter Q *doe* to *do* 30 times. The case for the Q copy-text does not rest on the fact that none of the 4 E settings of *doe* occurs at the point where Q sets its solitary *do* (for the odds are against such qualitative coincidence). Instead, we may argue quantitatively that the four times that E is persuaded by his copy to forsake his strong preference for *do* coincide with the proposition that the copy-text had as a characteristic a major

if not invariable preference for *doe*. It is unlikely that E
would have set so many examples of *doe* if the copy-text had
been relatively mixed. This argument is based purely on the
quantity of non-preferential forms that appear, without
regard for their position in relation to the corresponding
readings of the inferred copy-text. This quantitative analysis
is the only one that can be used when the copy-text being
tested is very strongly in favour of a particular spelling form
that disagrees with the preference of the compositor of the
reprint. Of the two orders of evidence, the quantitative is the
less valuable because it is grounded wholly on inference and
is very general in its application. However, the accumulation
of such evidence is not to be ignored.

On the other hand, qualitative evidence is used when the
critic can show not only that the compositor of the disputed
text under the influence of copy sets accidentals forms
variant from his usual practice, but also that these variants
from his usual preference seldom if ever appear except when
the corresponding non-preferential form is present in a copy-
text that has reasonably mixed characteristics in respect to
the variant being analysed. In *Othello* the treatment of *here*
is a partial example in that significance can be given to the
fact that, frequent as were the appearances of the uncharacteristic *here* spelling in the Folio (3 to 1, in fact), none
occurred in contradiction to the 2 examples in the Quarto of
E's preferential *heere*. Another example concerns the Folio
treatment of *heauen* and *Heauen*, where we may take it as
significant that in the 6 occurrences of the word, none of the
3 Folio lower-case forms appeared in the single place that the
Quarto set the more characteristic capitalized *Heauen*. Again,
once E's general preference for *honour* is established, the fact
would seem to be evidential that the single time we find
honor in F it coincides with one of the two *honor* spellings in
Q, and not with the one time that Q spells *honour*.

In *Othello* the qualitative argument needs to be a little
fine-spun because of the small amount of material available

for analysis in the six pages set by Compositor E. But better illustrations appear in the control texts. If one were analysing *Titus* Q3 as the copy-text for F, one would direct attention to the qualitative evidence that 3 of the 4 non-preferential *here* forms found in the Folio agree with 3 of the 14 occurrences of the short form in Q3 and only 1 of the 4 clashes with any of the 65 long *heere* forms in the Quarto. In the Folio none of the 39 uncharacteristic *doe* spellings reproduced in *Titus* agrees with any of the 25 *do* spellings in the Quarto. In *Romeo and Juliet* only 1 of the 14 long *doe* spellings appears as setting any of the 44 short forms present in Q3, and none of the 16 long *goe* spellings appears as a substitute for any of the 51 Q3 short forms. The odds from such examples can be calculated to demonstrate the validity of this kind of qualitative evidence. That quantitative evidence is also valid can be demonstrated by the example of the effect of copy on Compositor E in respect to *do*, *go*, and *here*. When the copy-text, like *Romeo*, is in strong general agreement with his preferential spellings, he is led to alter a larger number of non-preferential forms than when, as in *Titus*, the copy runs strongly against his own habits and he is correspondingly affected.

The distinction between quantitative and qualitative evidence and the evaluation of their respective weight has not been commonly made by textual critics; but such a differentiation is very useful indeed, especially when dealing, as in *Othello*, with a comparatively small quantity of text where in any given instance chance might be thought to explain the evidence as satisfactorily as design. That is, that Compositor E set *Titus Andronicus* from Q3, and *Romeo and Juliet* from Q3, can be demonstrated from substantive readings (since each case is an uncomplicated reprint), but if necessary the demonstration could also have been made by copious evidence from the accidentals, both by quantitative and by qualitative analysis. Whereas a critic might not be willing to accept the spelling evidence of any one word as conclusive, the pyramiding of the force of the qualitative evidence is very rapid indeed, and might be thought conclusive from the evidence even of two well-established balanced words.

In *Othello* where the evidence in E's stint must perforce be more delicate than in *Titus* or *Romeo*, the full force of the qualitative can be understood when it is not confused with the less precise quantitative evidence. Only by this separation can the leverage exerted by full qualitative concurrence within a series be appreciated as forming a cumulative broad unit so consistent in its coincidences with the special mixed features of the Q copy-text that chance must finally be ruled out as an operative force. Once the necessary compositor studies have been made, the rigorous application of this evidence, in place of the conventional impressionistic studies (or the unanalysed raw statistical studies), may hopefully lead to a final determination of disputed printed versus manuscript copy in the Folio.

Beyond that, with still further refinements made possible by the use of large electronic computers, it is not inconceivable that we may progress to an attempt to determine with superior precision to the present the more or less exact nature of certain manuscript printer's copy behind the authoritative quartos as well as the plays first printed in the Folio. Indeed, that some demonstrable features of Shakespeare's holographs may eventually be recovered from the prints is not entirely a dream.

NOTES

Note A, p. 159. This statement implies that the theatrical company, or the Folio editors, supplied the printer with the 'corrected' copy. But we have no right to assume such a process, at least as the norm. It may be that the editors sent a manuscript to the printer, who himself had the quarto brought into general conformity with the manuscript in order to provide his compositors with printed copy, as is tempting to conjecture happened with certain bad-quarto texts. However, in favour of the assumption that some of the annotated quartos of this second good group originated in the playhouse is this: in at least two of these texts the Folio version seems to be more theatrical in its form than the Quarto and may represent the text of the prompt-book, which the company would be unwilling to send to the printer. On the whole, a critic can speculate more reasonably with good texts than with bad that the company could have provided the annotated printed copy for Jaggard.

Note B, p. 162. For the usefulness of printed copy in connexion with setting from manuscript, see 'The Textual Relation of Q2 to Q1 *Hamlet*', *Studies in Bibliography*, viii (1956), 39–66. In some respects Roberts's consultation of Q1 to assist in deciphering the text of a difficult manuscript suggests what should be the modern critical point of view about the effect on the text of the conflation in the printer's shop of two textual sources. That is, so long as one could believe in the annotation of Q1 to serve as printer's copy for Act I of Q2, one could theorize that the annotation was performed in the theatre by an agent of the company. Such an origin could open the door to further theorizing about the effect on the text of a comparison made by someone familiar with the play and thus tempted at times to rely on his own memory, instead of the manuscript, to correct the print. But if the annotation were confined to the printer's shop (or if consultation on the order of Roberts's can be established), then the case is altered. The comparison may not be exact but it will be naïve, and there will be small chance that the scribe will write in what he thinks should be the correct text instead of what he thinks he sees in the manuscript. Variation will be inadvertent, therefore, and sophistication largely non-existent. The critical treatment of the text will be correspondingly affected.

Note C, p. 166. That is, if B is set from A, C from B, and D from C, there are only three basic situations:

	A	B	C	D
(1)	is	was	was	was
(2)	is	was	is	is
(3)	is	is	was	was

In the first, whether D was set from B or from C is not to be determined. In the second, C (and therefore D) has reverted to the original reading, probably on the basis of sense; but whether D was set from A or from C is in question, or indeed whether D was set from B but its compositor independently made the same corrections as did the C compositor. Only in the third series is it clear that the two touching editions are related.

If both C and D were independently set from B, we should have:

	A	B	C	D
(1)	is	was	was	was
(2)	is	is	was	is
(3)	is	was	were	was

Here no one can know in the first whether D was set from B or from C. In the second, D might be set from A or from B. Only in the uncommon situation represented by the third can one show that D derived from B. The difference between the rareness of no. 3 in this series when the related editions are not touching, and the commonness of no. 3 in the first series when the editions are touching, is the indication of the ease with which positive evidence can be found, or the considerable difficulty, according to the conditions. In the latter circumstance, most of the evidence must be negative and cumulative.

Note D, p. 166. Once intermediate editions are eliminated by negative evidence, the two remaining possibilities can be treated as if they were a touching series. What can correspond to C (although it may be H) must derive from A (which might be D) or from B (which might be F). If C derives from B, then the only significant series will be:

A	B	C
is	was	was
(is	was	were ?)

H(C) will be set from F(B), without regard for the fact that E and G could also read *was*, provided that negative evidence has eliminated E and G. If C derives from A, the only significant series will be:

A	B	C
is	was	is
(is	was	be ?)

H(C) will be set from D(A), even though E, G read *is*.

Note E, p.182. Dr. Walker isolates three nonce words in QF (*moraller, probal, exsufflicate*), of which two appear in identical spellings in both texts. She admits, rightly, 'It might be argued that their unfamiliarity encouraged copyists and compositors to preserve them as they found them, but this explanation will not account for the identical spelling of more common words which could be spelt in a number of ways.' She then selects *morties* (i.e., mortise), 'though half a dozen spellings were possible'; *lushious* 'as against "luscious" in the Folio text of *A Midsummer Night's Dream* is again common to the printed texts'; so too is *Pyoners* 'as against "Pioners" in the Folio text of *Henry V* and all three texts of *Hamlet*'. This evidence does not get us very far. In fact, *luscious* appears only twice in Shakespeare. That Compositor E spells it *lushious* (as does Q) cannot therefore be utilized to show the nature of his copy, since *luscious* in the *Dream* was set by a different compositor. Correspondingly, *Pioners* in *Henry V* and in *Hamlet* was set by Compositor A; thus whether in setting *Pyoners* Compositor B was following Q's copy or using his natural spelling cannot be determined. Only in B's *morties* can any sort of comparison be made: for what it is worth, in *Hamlet* B once set Q2 *morteist* (if Q2 were the copy) as *mortiz'd*. Yet this single occurrence cannot establish whether or not he might have had other spellings, one of which was *morties* as in *Othello*. Dr. Walker then quotes *Othello*, IV. ii. 57–64, and comments: 'The Folio reads "garnerd", "dries", "heere" and emends "thy" to "thou". We have, of course, to reckon with the fact that the *Othello* printed texts are contemporaries. The compositors of Okes (the Quarto printer) and Jaggard have certain spelling conventions in common, and "heart", "beare", "fountaine", "keepe", "Cesterne", "complexion", "looke", "grim" and "hell" are normal Folio spellings; but others are what may be described as Folio variables: "currant", "runnes", "foule", "Toades" and "young" might well have been otherwise spelt without infringing such rules as existed in Jaggard's printing-house.' But only a moment's reflection is necessary to recognize that whether or not these words might have been spelled in a variety of ways by the four other Folio compositors, no evidence is being adduced that the identified Compositor B is or is not following copy in this passage. Only if it were shown (as it is not) that B was significantly influenced by his copy to go against his usual habits here and in some number of other passages could we admit an argument of this general nature. (The attempt below to put E's established characteristics up against the Quarto represents quite another order of evidence.) In Dr. Walker's *Textual Problems of the First Folio* (1953), p. 153, *pudled* is added as an anomaly passed on from Q to F. It is true that Compositor B, setting from manuscript in *The Comedy of Errors*, spells it *puddled*; but again one swallow does not make a summer and we have no means of knowing whether his spelling of this word was indifferent or whether he was following copy in either text. As for *timerous*, also put forward, E nowhere else sets this word, and hence whether this is his typical spelling cannot be determined. (Arguments in spelling tests from analogy are always dangerous, and so it may or may not be significant that in *Romeo*, II. i. 31, E follows copy in setting the spelling *Humerous*.) Finally, in pp. 153–6 it is noticed that the spelling of weak verbs with -*t* or -*'d* in preterite and past participle is significantly similar in the two texts. The Quarto and Folio both agree in -*t* spellings on 24 occasions, in -*'d* spellings on 25 occasions, and differ on 23 occasions when Q has -*t* but F has -*'d* or -*ed*. Once more the evidence adduced from other plays about variable practice is not associated with identified compositors, and therefore is suspect, despite Sir Walter Greg's singling-out of this as the clinching evidence for the association of the two texts (*The Shakespeare First Folio* (1955), p. 363) although the other spelling evidence adduced seemed to him to be weak. When the spellings associated with Compositor E are surveyed, the evidence of his section proves to have little if any primary value. In his stint Q has 7 -*t* endings, 4 of which are duplicated in F. However, one of these, *capt*, does not appear elsewhere in Shakespeare. The second, *stufft*, comes twice in E's setting of *Romeo and Juliet* where E is following his copy and hence we have no means of knowing whether he did or did not prefer this spelling. The third and fourth are *past* (for *pass'd*), which comes under the same stricture, for E follows his copy *past* twice in *Titus* and once in *Romeo*. Hence E's personal characteristics for these words cannot be determined, and in these circumstances no conjecture about the influence of copy on his forms in *Othello* is permissible. In the remaining three cases he spelled Q -*t* (*blest*, *blusht*, *wisht*) with -*'d* and he once set *profest* from manuscript. Since E often followed copy in -*t* but also had some tendency to change to -*'d*, it is not necessarily significant that in none of the few remaining possibilities does he set Q -*'d* as -*ed* or as -*t*. As Greg indicated, in the *Othello* argument the random notice of unusual spellings as evidence for the genetic relationship of two texts is not sound practice, at least when such evidence is adduced as primary and not as merely supplementary to a case already well on the way to being established by other means.

Note F, p. 192. In fact, the one serious piece of evidence in *Othello* against Q as copy-text for F concerns E's treatment of the -*y* endings. In *Titus* and in *Romeo* he has a tendency to follow copy, but any change will definitely be in the direction of shortening -*ie* to -*y*. The large number of words in *Othello* in which -*y* would have been lengthened to -*ie* if Q were the copy certainly runs contrary to the practice observed in the control texts. It is likely, however, that this treatment of -*y* and -*ie* according to the preceding consonant was a developing characteristic with E, and one that might be traced in E's share of *Hamlet* and *King Lear* (which intervene between the control texts and *Othello*). Certainly such an alteration of characteristics may be observed in another word in *Hamlet* and *King Lear* with the result that evidence in *Othello* at first sight contrary to the Q copy-text hypothesis may be shown to be neutral after all. The example is the exclamation *O* or *Oh*, which in *Titus* and in *Romeo* is irregularly spelled but the copy-text form invariably followed by E. Yet in *Othello*, wherein the Q is invariably O, the Folio prints O only once but *Oh* 7 times. Nevertheless, despite the evidence of *Titus* and of *Romeo*, in *King Lear*, regardless of the quarto serving as copy, E develops a tendency to alter O to *Oh* and the same process may be observed in *Hamlet* if we assume that Q2 was the copy-text. The *Oh* spellings in F *Othello* contrary to Quarto O would seem to have no significance, therefore.

INDEX

'accidentals', definition of, 2.

acting, Elizabethan, 149–50, 161.

actor's reconstruction, 15, 146, 149–50, 153.

Alexander, Peter, 165, 168 n.

Aristippus, 143.

Banks, John, 152.

Beaumont and Fletcher, 160.

bibliography: modern developments in, 5–7, 58, 63; definition of (analytical), 24–26, (textual) 7–8, 11, 26–30, (descriptive) 24, 27, 34; limited authority of textual bibliographer, 53–59; as a scientific method, 71–74. *See* literary criticism.

Bolton, J. S. G., 146 n.

book-keeper, 149–51, 157, 161.

Bowers, Fredson, 1 n., 2 n., 10 n., 17 n., 23 n., 25 n., 38 n., 41 n., 49 n., 62, 71 n., 73 n., 84 n., 108 n., 118, 119 n., 122 n., 126 n., 128 n., 141 n., 143 n., 152 n., 198.

Brown, Arthur, 2 n.

Brown, John Russell, 2 n., 38 n., 73 n., 94, 122 n.

Cairncross, A. S., 41, 60, 145 n., 162 n., 190 n.

cancels, 68, 77–78, 80–84, 96, 118–20, 127–8, 131–2, 142–5, 152.

Cantrell, P. L., 144 n.

Chambers, Sir Edmund, 77.

Christs Passion, 84 n.

collimated light, 25, 83; *see also* Povey-Martin lamp.

Comedy of Errors, 200.

compositor: characteristics of, 8–9, 12–13, 42–44, 53–54, 93–95, 133–5, 149, 164; traditional methods of, 66–67, 73; speed of, 99–100; uniqueness of each compositor, 33–34; errors of, 14, 41, 58–59, 67–68, 92, 113, 123, 145, 153–4, 162, 164; whether proofreader or compositor responsible for errors, 69–70, 90, 111, 120–5, 128–9; importance of identification, 12–13,

37–38, 53–54, 93–95; identification of Folio compositors, 12, 42–44, 50, 93–94, 154–6.

Compositor A, 30, 42, 50, 54 n., 62, 94, 141–2, 154, 167–8, 179–81, 183, 189 n., 199.

Compositor B, 30, 42, 50, 94, 98 n., 133, 145, 154–6, 164 n., 179–81, 183, 189 n., 191, 199–200.

Compositor C, 42, 62, 179, 181.

Compositor D, 42, 62.

Compositor E, 42, 94, 126 n., 145, 155–7, 164 n., 179–97, 199–201.

Congreve, W., 84, 152.

Copy for the Folio Text of Richard III, 77 n.

Coriolanus, 54 n., 180.

Country Wit, 84 n.

Crane, Ralph, 137–8, 160.

Crowne, John, 84 n.

Cyrus the Great, 152, 155.

Daiches, David, 61.

Daniel, P. A., 172.

Dekker, T., 9, 13, 15–18, 20, 26 n., 28, 32, 51, 70, 77, 88, 101, 103 n., 106, 120–6, 131, 133 n., 155 n.

Dickins, Bruce, 62.

Disappointment, 152.

distribution of type, 66, 69, 80, 110, 142–3.

Divine Poems, 90, 92.

Doctor Faustus, 48.

Donne, John, 90.

Double Dealer, 84, 152.

Dryden, J., 48, 118, 127, 152, 162 n., 163 n., 167.

The Dumb Knight, 77, 84.

Duthie, G. I., 146.

eclecticism, 18, 22, 23 & n., 32, 147.

Edwards, Philip, 155 n.

eighteenth-century literature, editing of, 47, 61–62.

Elizabethan Plays (1933), 18.

Elizabethan Stage, 78 n.

PRINTED IN GREAT BRITAIN
AT THE UNIVERSITY PRESS, OXFORD
BY VIVIAN RIDLER
PRINTER TO THE UNIVERSITY